MALAY KINSHIP AND MARRIAGE
IN SINGAPORE

LONDON SCHOOL OF ECONOMICS
MONOGRAPHS ON SOCIAL ANTHROPOLOGY
NO. 21

Malay Kinship and Marriage in Singapore

by

JUDITH DJAMOUR

UNIVERSITY OF LONDON
THE ATHLONE PRESS
NEW YORK: HUMANITIES PRESS INC

First published in 1959 *by*
THE ATHLONE PRESS
UNIVERSITY OF LONDON
at 2 *Gower Street, London,* WC1

Distributed by Constable & Co *Ltd*
12 *Orange Street, London,* WC2

Canada
Oxford University Press
Toronto

Reprinted with corrections 1965

Library of Congress Catalog Card No. 65–17937

First printed in 1959 *by*
ROBERT CUNNINGHAM AND SONS LTD
ALVA

Reprinted in 1965 *by photo-litho by*
WILLIAM CLOWES AND SONS LTD
BECCLES

Preface

THIS book is a very shortened version of a thesis submitted for the degree of Ph.D. in the University of London. Several chapters of it, in a somewhat different form, were part of a Report to the Colonial Social Science Research Council on fieldwork I carried out under its auspices from January 1949 to November 1950 in Singapore.[1] The title of the Report was *The Family Structure of the Singapore Malays*.

Most of the material contained in the section on Adoption in Chapter 5 has been published as an article, 'Adoption of Children Among Singapore Malaysians', in the *Journal of the Royal Anthropological Institute*, vol. lxxxii, Part II, 1952.

I wish to acknowledge here with deep gratitude the great help, guidance, and advice I received from my supervisor, Professor Raymond Firth, in analysing the material collected in the field and in the writing up of the thesis upon which this work is based.

My husband, Dr Maurice Freedman, was in Singapore during the same period and under the same auspices, carrying out fieldwork on Chinese family organization. I have benefited greatly from discussions we had both during the period of the research itself and later. I am also very grateful to him for his valuable suggestions and critical comments on the typescript.

In 1954 my husband and I spent some months in Indonesia, in the course of which we carried out brief investigations of the social organization of two areas of Java and a Minangkabau village in Sumatra. I incidentally refer to some of the Indonesian material we gathered.

London,   J. D.
July 1958

[1] See the recommendations in Professor Raymond Firth's *Report on Social Science Research in Malaya*, Singapore 1948, pp. 33-4.

Contents

INTRODUCTION   1

1. THE STRUCTURE OF SINGAPORE MALAY SOCIETY   3

2. KINSHIP   23

3. THE HOUSEHOLD   52

4. MARRIAGE   66

5. CHILDREN: BIRTH, ADOPTION, SOCIALIZATION   88

6. DIVORCE   110

7. CONCLUSION   141

LIST OF WORKS CITED   148

INDEX   150

Introduction

I WENT to Singapore in January 1949 and left at the end of November 1950. The main period of fieldwork was divided almost equally between a fishing community on the south-west coast and an urban area. I also spent two months in an exclusively Malay suburb known as the Malay Settlement. The inhabitants of the fishing village—which I call Tanjong— were local Malays, whereas the Malays in the urban and suburban areas were a mixed local-Malay and immigrant-Indonesian group, with a preponderance in the number of immigrants. Tanjong was an isolated village of just over two hundred inhabitants; the population had been principally engaged in fishing for many generations; it was entirely Malay, with the exception of the five shopkeepers, one of whom was Chinese and the others Malabari Muslims. The urban area where I lived had a mixed Malay, Chinese, and Indian population, living in quarters built by the Singapore Improvement Trust; the Malay population there was made up of the households of labourers and semi-skilled workers, with a sprinkling of skilled workers, office messengers, and junior clerks. The Malay Settlement had a very mixed occupational pattern: its inhabitants included labourers, skilled and semi-skilled workers, small tradesmen; and a number of civil servants, schoolteachers and clerks. I rented a small room in a house accommodating several Malay households.

Apart from intensive fieldwork in these three areas I established contact with, and visited regularly, descendants of the Singapore Royal Family as well as several households of schoolteachers and clerks in different areas of the Colony.

I used Malay as the language medium and employed no interpreters or assistants.

In this book my aim is to make an analysis of the structure of Malay kinship and marriage in Singapore on the basis of my research there. I deal exclusively with conditions during the two years 1949-50.

When I went to the field I had no specific major theory which I wanted to test, but I was particularly interested in the problem of the instability of Malay marriage and in the effects which this instability had on the divorced couples themselves, on their children, and on their respective kinsmen. Some obvious points I had to consider were the transfer of property at marriage and at divorce, the pattern of residence, the custody of the children, and the facility of remarrying.

I also knew that Malays in the Island had been for several generations an economically depressed minority; that they had no official political representation as Malays, but only (together with Indians and Arabs) as Muslims; that they had little or no effective community organization; and no tribal, clan or lineage organization whatsoever. These facts led me to the conclusion that it was important to determine whether in contrast to the lack of formal corporate groupings there might not be special types of economic solidarity of an informal nature between a person and his close kinsmen.

A few months after I arrived in the Colony I became interested in a third problem, that of the transfer of young children, and I realized that the institution of adoption formed an integral part of Malay family organization; 'integral' because if the institution did not exist, family organization would, I think, be different.

I

The Structure of Singapore Malay Society

SINGAPORE is a political unit made up of a conglomeration of diverse cultural elements. In 1819 it was acquired by Sir Stamford Raffles on behalf of the East India Company from the Sultan of Johore.[1] The Colony in 1950 included Christmas Island and the Cocos-Keeling Islands. The last published Census, in 1947, gave the distribution of the population as follows:

Chinese	730,133
Malays	72,154
Other Malaysians	43,581
Indians	68,978
Europeans	9,351
Eurasians	9,110
Other Communities	7,517
Total	940,824

DEMOGRAPHICAL POSITION OF THE MALAYS

No exact figures are available of the Island's population when Raffles landed in January 1819, but it is generally believed that there were fewer than two hundred souls at the time. Among them was the representative of the Sultan of Johore, whose title was that of Těměnggong, with his suite. It is said that even at this early date there were some Chinese inhabitants on the Island. Hayes Marriott, writing in *One Hundred Years of Singapore*,[2] says that at its foundation 'the population amounted to about 150 individuals. . . . About thirty of them were Chinese and the rest Malays, who had accompanied the Temenggong when he settled in Singapore

[1] The State of Johore belonged to the Riau-Lingga dynasty, and it included the Island of Singapore. Before Raffles landed at Singapore the younger son of the late Riau-Lingga ruler had proclaimed himself Sultan of Johore during the temporary absence of his older brother, Těngku Hussein. Raffles sent to Riau for Těngku Hussein, acknowledged him as Sultan of Johore, and signed with him a treaty granting the British the right to settle on the Island of Singapore. See F. Swettenham, *British Malaya*, London 1948, pp. 60-70; and C. O. Blagden, 'The Foundation of the Settlement' in *One Hundred Years of Singapore*, edited by W. Makepeace, G. E. Brooke, and R. St. J. Braddell, 2 vols., London 1921, vol. i, pp. 8-10. See also *Hikajat Abdullah*, edited by R. A. Datoek Besar and R. Roolvink, Djakarta, Amsterdam 1953, pp. 288-93.   [2] op. cit., vol. i, p. 341.

in 1811'. He adds that in January 1824 the first census was taken and that there were then 4,580 Malays and 3,317 Chinese. There was a steady and spectacular increase of Chinese immigrants—largely male—in the course of the following years. From 1836 onwards, Singapore-born Malays and Javanese, Boyanese, and Bugis immigrants have been as a group greatly outnumbered by the Chinese.

Singapore nowadays has two types of Malay inhabitants:

1. Malays who have lived in the Colony for several generations or have moved there from the Peninsula.

2. Immigrants from Indonesia (mainly Java and Bawean) who have been settled in the Island for one, two or three generations.

Mr Del Tufo in the 1947 Census Report refers to the former as 'Malays' and the latter as 'Other Malaysians'. He states in his chapter on *Race*[1] that enumerators were instructed to accept the statement made by the person questioned (unless it was obviously absurd or impossible), especially if it was made before witnesses, as usually happens in villages. 'Very few Indonesian immigrants, for instance, would claim to be Malays unless they were accepted as such by the village community.'

There is a notable excess of males over females in both groups, but the excess is absolutely and proportionately greater in the case of the immigrant community. Thus:

Malays: 38,182 males; 33,972 females
Other Malaysians: 25,066 males; 18,515 females

In the case of Other Malaysians the excess of males over females is largely due to the fact that male immigration of Indonesians largely exceeds female immigration. The sex-distribution of *Singapore-born* Other Malaysians is almost equal (11,443 males and 11,716 females). Where indigenous Malays are concerned the explanation is that there was a net excess of 5,144 males over females born in the Federation and enumerated in Singapore. On the other hand there was an excess of only 450 females over males among the total number of Malays born in Singapore but enumerated in the Federation.[2] A glance at the sex distribution by main age-groups[3] shows that for both local and immigrant Malays the excess of males occurs most strikingly among young adults, who are of course the most mobile:

	MALAYS		OTHER MALAYSIANS	
Age	*Males*	*Females*	*Males*	*Females*
Under 15 years	12,991	13,949	7,455	7,688
15—44 years	21,703	16,892	13,666	8,772
44 years and over	3,488	3,131	3,945	2,055
Total all ages	38,182	33,972	25,066	18,515

[1] M. V. Del Tufo, *A Report on the 1947 Census of Population, Malaya*, London and Singapore, 1950, p. 71.
[2] See *A Report on the 1947 Census of Population, Malaya*; tables relating to birthplace versus place of enumeration, pp. 310-21.   [3] ibid., p. 176.

OCCUPATION

The main occupations of Singapore Malays are those of skilled and semi-skilled work in transport and communication, metal factories and electricity; fishing; general unskilled labour; Police and Army Other Ranks; personal service, clerks and typists. Other Malaysians are engaged in the same main types of occupations but not always in the same proportions. Only a negligible number of immigrants work as fishermen, as Police or Army Other Ranks, or as clerks. They are concentrated in transport and communication, unskilled labour and agriculture. The statement which follows gives the main categories in which the population is gainfully employed.[1]

GAINFUL OCCUPATION	MALAYS		OTHER MALAYSIANS	
	Males	Females	Males	Females
Fishing	1,659	24	75	—
Agriculture	632	162	2,427	114
Metal Workers	1,214	10	685	5
Electricians[2]	735	1	329	2
Transport and communication	7,243	39	5,780	21
Workers in Wood and furniture	310	4	181	2
Commercial and Financial	535	67	827	40
Public Administration	4,056	2	168	—
Professional Occupations	386	116	221	36
Personal Service	692	419	561	478
Clerks and Draughtsmen, Typists	1,313	16	232	5
Unskilled Workers	2,513	137	3,524	44
Total	21,298	991	15,010	747
Other occupations	2,185	109	1,472	59
The total gainfully occupied population is 41,861:	23,473	1,100	16,482	806

The balance in 'other occupations' is made up of small numbers of workers in textile goods, printing, building and decoration, warehouses, fire-fighting, etc. and of others in unspecified occupations.

In agriculture, whereas Malays are mainly fruit and vegetable growers and coconut cultivators, Other Malaysians are mainly fruit and vegetable growers and rubber cultivators. In metal work, both groups are mainly fitters and motor mechanics. In transport and communication, a large proportion of both groups are employed in road and water transport. In commerce, both groups are mainly occupied in retail business and hawking. In public administration, both groups are mainly Police and Army Other

[1] For full details, see Census Report for 1947, pp. 519-24.
[2] It is surprising to find Malay women employed as electricians. The Census Report also shows (p. 520) that in the Chinese group there are six women similarly employed and in the Indian group two women.

Ranks. In professional occupations, both groups are mainly ancillary medical personnel and teachers. In personal service, they are mainly domestic servants.

In both groups only a very small proportion of women are gainfully occupied: 3·2 per cent of the total Malay female population (1,100 out of 33,972), and 4·4 per cent of the total Other Malaysian female population (806 out of 18,515).[1] In both groups also, women are primarily engaged in personal service, while a comparatively smaller number of them are engaged in agriculture, teaching, hawking and unskilled labour.

As far as the present study is concerned, the same broad general principles apply both to indigenous and immigrant Malays. Therefore I shall use the term 'Malays' to refer to both groups. Whenever specific points of difference arise, however, I shall draw attention to them. It is worth noting here that both groups are Muslim, are physically indistinguishable, eat the same food cooked in much the same way, and consider themselves as forming one single community which can be sharply distinguished from other Singapore resident communities such as Chinese, Indians, Europeans or Eurasians.

As for dress, the men of both groups usually wear European clothes (trousers and a shirt) at work, and Malay clothes (sarong and *baju*) at home. On most ceremonial occasions, however, men frequently wear full Malay dress which consists of a *baju* and a pair of long loose trousers, and a sarong around the waist, over the trousers. Their *baju* is a loose fitting blouse with long sleeves, fastened at the neck. There are variations of this general pattern, some men wearing a sarong and shirt at work or at home, for instance. As head-dress men usually wear a *songkok*, a cap made of velvet almost always black in colour.

There is some differentiation in the style of clothes worn by local and immigrant women. The former usually wear over their sarong a *baju kurong*, a very long loose blouse fastened at the neck. Immigrant women, particularly first-generation Indonesians, wear a *baju kĕbaya* which fits tightly, is open down the front, and is fastened in the centre with a series of three brooches called *kĕrongsang*. However, I saw many cases of local women wearing a *baju kĕbaya* and of immigrant women wearing the *baju kurong*. The women of both groups wear a long narrow scarf (*sĕlendang*) over their hair when they go out. Their faces are not veiled.[2]

As footwear, men use Western-style shoes or sandals, especially for work in town, and Malay-type open slippers. Women use mules with flat

---

[1] Percentages are given to the nearest first place of decimals.

[2] I was told that several decades ago Malay women wore in the street a sarong to cover their head and shoulders and partly conceal their faces from view. In 1950 one could very occasionally see an elderly Malay or Arab woman using this form of dress out-of-doors. A physician who visited Malaya a century ago stated: ' . . . the Mussulman women are generally veiled . . . they throw their dresses over their heads. . . .' Dr Yvan, *Six Months Among the Malays and a Year in China*, London 1855, p. 7.

or high heels. At home, however, and when visiting indoors both men and women go barefoot.

The Island of Singapore and adjacent islets cover an area of approximately 217 square miles, and Malays live in many different parts of it. They are found in densely populated urban districts, living close to Chinese and Indians; and in suburbs of the town, sometimes again near inhabitants of other ethnic groups and sometimes in exclusively Malay districts such as the Malay Settlement. In the rural areas, however, Malays usually live in small homogeneous communities.

Communication between the various parts of the Colony is by means of buses, trishaws, and bicycles. In 1950 only a handful of Malays owned motor cars. The women and children travelled mainly by bus in the country, and by bus or trishaw in the town. Trishaws rarely operated outside the municipal area. The men used bicycles as well as buses and trishaws. In Malay villages on the coast the men were often fishermen and owned small boats which they also used for visits to other coastal villages or to the small islets off the mainland. In some villages built well away from the main road, close to a rubber plantation or to the seashore, there was no regular means of public transport; men who did not own bicycles had to walk several miles to the nearest bus stop. In some cases villagers paid a few cents to ride on the lorry which came daily to the village to bring the local shopkeeper's supplies or to fetch the fish catch for marketing.

Malays living in suburbs or in the city itself engaged in varied occupations, ranging from office messengers, drivers, domestic servants, labourers, mechanics, hawkers, and postmen, to clerks and schoolteachers. In such districts the population was fluid. The majority of Malays did not own the rooms or houses in which they lived but rented them from Chinese, Arab, or Indian landlords. If other accommodation was available nearer to the chief wage-earner's place of work, the household moved. In the villages, on the other hand, most Malays owned the houses they occupied.

Singapore Malays said that ideally they liked to live in a wooden house built on stilts, with a verandah, a front room for receiving guests, one or two bedrooms, and a kitchen; there must be two entrances, a front and a kitchen entrance. On the occasions when both male and female guests were expected, such as weddings or religious festivals, the men would use the front entrance and the women the kitchen entrance. In the rural areas and in the suburbs of Singapore town a few Malays did in fact live in this type of house. Poorer houses often had no verandah but only an open platform consisting of a few planks, and only one room apart from the kitchen; they were built without skilled help by the owner with the aid of his kinsmen.

In the case of Army and Police personnel and labourers of the Municipality or Harbour Board, and in some other cases, quarters were usually provided by the employers. The accommodation was built on ground level in the shape of lines or blocks, every household being allocated a self-contained unit of one or two rooms, a kitchen, lavatory and bathroom.

There were also owners and so-called 'chief tenants' of larger houses who rented out rooms to individual households. In such cases there was often only one kitchen shared by all for cooking purposes, but meals were eaten in the room which the household occupied. This type of housing arrangement was common in the urban area with its very dense population. Clerks, teachers, skilled and semi-skilled workmen, labourers, drivers, shop assistants, often lived each one with his household in a rented room. Singapore Malays showed a strong preference for accommodation in a house which let or sub-let to Malays only.

EDUCATION

Education in Malay vernacular schools was free. In 1949 there were thirty-nine Malay schools in the Island.[1] The teachers were Malays, the medium of instruction the Malay language, and although in principle any Singapore child could attend a Government vernacular school, in fact the pupils were almost exclusively Malay. Chinese and Indian parents showed little desire to educate their children in the Malay language only. Of the thirty-nine Malay schools, nine were for girls only, nine were for boys only, and twenty-one were mixed. It appeared from conversations I had with senior officials of the Department of Education that Malay mixed schools were not established as an experiment in co-education; but in some cases on account of a shortage of buildings and teachers, and in other cases—such as in small isolated villages and islands—because the total student population was too small to justify the expense of separate schools for boys and girls. The tendency in mixed schools was for boys and girls to play separately during breaks. Teachers in girls' schools were women, while those in mixed and in boys' schools were men.

In 1949 the total enrolment was 7,862 pupils in Malay schools: 5,443 boys and 2,419 girls. Children usually went to school at the age of six and left when they were thirteen to fifteen years old. Many pupils had been greatly retarded by the war, as the system of education was dislocated by the Japanese Occupation. Before the war, school attendance was during mornings only. In 1949 and 1950, because of the shortage of school buildings and the increase in the student population, some school buildings were used both mornings and afternoons for different groups of pupils and teachers.

Few Malays had any education in English. Up to 1950 the practice was to select only these pupils who had successfully passed Standard IV in the vernacular school and were under the age of twelve for admission to Government English schools. There were eighteen mission schools in the Colony—in receipt of Government subsidies—but less than a handful of Malays attended them; parents were reluctant to send their children lest

[1] See *Colony of Singapore Annual Report, 1949*, p. 69.

they became converts to Christianity. The overwhelming bulk of the student population of mission schools was therefore Chinese, Eurasian, and Indian.

No religious tuition was given in Government Malay schools and it was common for pupils to attend private Koran classes several hours a week. There were also some so-called 'Arabic schools' in the Colony which were primarily religious schools but gave some tuition in elementary arithmetic and in the Arabic language.

The 1947 Census[1] gives some interesting figures on literacy. For the Singapore Malay population in general, including the indigenous and immigrant groups aged fifteen and over, the rates were per mille (1931 Census rates shown in brackets):

Males	Females	Persons
677 (398)	201 (80)	478 (265)

The rate of literacy per mille in English ('the test was ability to read and write a simple letter in the language and the reply restricted to "yes" or "no" ') for the same age-group was, of course, much lower:

	Males	Females	Persons
Malays	193	18	115
Other Malaysians	62	9·4	42

The comparative figures for the two groups (also aged fifteen and over) taken together in the 1931 Census were:

Males	Females	Persons
101	7	59

The fact that only a small proportion of the Malay working population was literate in English severely restricted the scope within which they could seek paid employment. Clerical and administrative jobs in most commercial concerns and in Government service required a fairly good knowledge of English (certainly more knowledge than for the Census test) and in 1950, therefore, the majority of Malays employed in such offices were messengers and office boys. It sometimes happened that two brothers had widely different occupations, one as a senior clerk earning $250[2] a month and another as a driver with a monthly wage of $80, mainly because the latter's entire schooling was in Malay. Parents generally recognized that literacy in English was the greatest single asset for obtaining a well-paid post with chances of promotion and they were therefore increasingly eager to send their children—especially their boys—to English schools.

It is only in recent decades that Malays have agreed to send their daughters to school and in 1950 there were still many conservative parents who sent their sons to Government schools and their daughters either to

---

[1] p. 95.
[2] The Malayan dollar is worth 2s. 4d. There are 100 cents in a dollar.

an Arabic school or only for an hour a day to the house of a Koran instructor. There was also a strong tendency, especially in the rural areas, to remove a girl from school when she reached puberty, or was about to reach it. On the other hand, there was one Government Malay Girls' School in the Municipal area which boasted a growing enrolment of pupils.

GENERAL ECONOMIC POSITION

Singapore Malays were acutely aware that they were an economically depressed group. They frequently commented upon this fact—whether they were fishermen, domestic servants, labourers, clerks, or teachers—and contrasted their status with that of the resident Chinese population. They willingly admitted that there were many very poor Chinese in the Colony; then they added: 'But look at the big houses and the large cars in Singapore. Whom do they belong to? To the Chinese. Of course some also belong to Europeans and Indians and Arabs, but the majority belong to the Chinese. Is there any Malay here who is as rich as that, any Malay living in a very big house with many servants, who owns a great deal of property and a large car? Not one.' On the other hand, most Malays readily stated that their community was not a rich one, partly because Malays are not good businessmen and are not sufficiently industrious in accumulating capital and investing it profitably: 'They do not like to work hard in order to acquire greater wealth, but prefer to spend what they earn, as they earn it.'

Singapore Malays and Chinese certainly appeared to have different cultural values. Singapore Chinese on the whole considered the acquisition of wealth to be one of the most important aims in life, and almost an end in itself; they were indefatigable workers and keen businessmen. Singapore Malays, on the other hand, attached great importance to easy and graceful living. Until very recently, the majority of them seemed content if they had a neat wooden house, sufficient food to eat, and a new suit of clothes for *hari raya*, the festival at the end of the Muslim fasting month of Ramadan.[1]

When I first came to live in Tanjong I enquired whether there were any Malay shops. The fishermen laughed loudly at me for asking such a question, and said there had never been a Malay shop in the district, only Chinese and Indian, because 'the Malays are too poor'. They explained that if one of them earned a dollar, he spent it on food, on smoking and on amusements. If a fisherman had landed a good catch he would buy a packet of ready-made cigarettes; if not, he would buy *rokok daun*.[2]

[1] cf. Sir Richard Winstedt ' . . . the Malay attitude that, though a necessity, work cannot be counted a virtue. What the European moralist regards as lost time, the Malay regards as time gained.' *The Malays, A Cultural History*, London 1950, p. 135.

[2] This consists of the dried leaf of the *nipah* palm which is used instead of cigarette paper and into which is rolled a cheap local tobacco, sometimes mixed with spices.

The subject of Malay improvidence attracted both fair and unfair comment from all other local inhabitants. On one occasion I told an Arab lady, who had been settled in the Colony for forty years, that many Malays had declared to me that they spent in the afternoon whatever sum they had earned on the same morning. The Arab lady remarked: 'It is my experience that many Malays go further. They spend today what they will earn tomorrow.'

In the urban area where I later went to live I noticed that Malay women used to buy their fish and vegetables daily for cash from Chinese hawkers, paying often about thirty per cent more than they would have paid at a market less than a mile away. They were aware of the difference, and would comment that it was too much trouble to go all the way to the market. In that district I had a neighbour whose husband was a lorry driver earning $120 a month. One day she told me cheerfully that she was very happy because her husband had found another job, driving a small van for $80 a month. It was a better job because it meant shorter hours than driving the lorry and was less tiring. It also meant that her husband came home earlier in the evenings and could have more leisure; this was much better than working until 9 or 10 p.m. on most evenings and earning $120 a month. What was the use of earning a larger salary if one could not rest and have some leisure? she asked. Moreover, driving the van dirtied his clothes less than driving the lorry and she would not have as much washing to do.

Since the end of the war there have been many attempts by Malay leaders in the Peninsula and Singapore to encourage a different attitude to wealth and to saving, using the industrious Chinese as a model. This campaign directly resulted from the rapidly increasing degree of political awareness of the Malays, and from their distress at the unfavourable comparison between their economic and educational achievements and those of the Chinese living among them.

INTERMARRIAGE

The number of Singapore Eurasians or Europeans who married Malays was negligible.

Intermarriage with Chinese

Marriage unions between Singapore Malays and Chinese were extremely rare. When they did occur, the match was usually between a Chinese girl who became converted to Islam—or rather, as the Malay phrase goes, *masok Mĕlayu*, became Malay (lit. 'enter Malay')—and a Malay man. I came across only three such unions, one in a rural area and two in the Municipality.[1]

---

[1] There were, of course, many more unions of this type in the Colony. One further remark is necessary. Some observers conclude, when they see a Chinese-looking woman married to a Malay, that she must have *masok Mĕlayu* as an adult

Marriage between a Malay woman and a Chinese—even when he had *masok Mĕlayu* to become eligible[1]—was even more infrequent. It was almost unheard of for a Malay, whether a man or a woman, to abjure Islam and marry a Chinese according to Chinese or Christian rites.[2]

Intermarriage with Indians[3]

The 1947 Census Report, unlike the 1931 Report, gives no figures for religion. Out of a total Singapore Indian population of 51,019 in 1931, the majority (31,121) were Hindus and over a quarter (13,330) Muslims. Of these 13,330 Muslim Indians, 11,609 were men. But in spite of the very uneven sex ratio, marriage between Muslim Indians and Malay women was rare.[4] It seemed that reluctance to enter into such unions mainly originated from the Malay community. Malays explained that it was in principle better to marry a person of one's own *bangsa* ('race')[5]; that an Indian might suddenly decide to return to his country and desert his wife or ask her to follow him, either of which courses would be unpleasant to the Malay wife; and that Indians did not allow their wives reasonable freedom of movement. Then again the conclusion would be drawn that it

in order to marry. In the majority of such cases, however, further enquiry reveals that the Chinese-looking woman was adopted from infancy by Malays, reared as a Malay girl, and considers herself a Malay. Were it not for her facial appearance, she would be otherwise indistinguishable in every respect from a Malay woman. See the section on adoption below, in chapter 5.

[1] Islam allows the Jewish or Christian bride to retain her religion; but if the bride-to-be is not a Muslim, or a Christian or a Jewess, she must become converted to Islam. On the other hand, a Muslim woman may marry only a Muslim: either a man born a Muslim or one converted to Islam.

[2] Some Chinese in the Colony are Christians. In Singapore in the period January 1941–August 1949 no Chinese was married to a Malay by Christian rites; 6 Malay men and 3 Malay women married Chinese according to civil rites, however. See M. Freedman, *Chinese Family and Marriage in Singapore*, H.M.S.O., London 1957, p. 125. It is of course possible that the parties married by civil rites were also married by Muslim rites.

[3] I follow here the 1947 Census which uses the word 'Indian' in its pre-Partition sense; it includes Muslims. According to this Census the total number of Indians in Singapore was 68,978. Their main occupations were in commerce; transport and communication (especially as drivers and dock labourers); personal service; and un-skilled labour. There were also groups of over 2,000 individuals each, employed as clerks and skilled workers.

[4] I base this statement upon personal observation, general comment on the part of Muslim Indians and Malays, and comments by Singapore *kathi* I interviewed. There were no entries relating to 'race' in Muslim marriage registers. See below, pp. 116f.

[5] In Tanjong there was only one Malay woman married to an Indian; he was one of the shopkeepers. The other Indian and Chinese shopkeepers had no wives or children in the village. I was told that the marriage had taken place during the war, and that extreme poverty had induced the woman to marry an Indian. I never saw her visit the houses of other villagers or entertain them, and her little boy wore a charm round the neck which, said the Indian father, had been made by a wise man of his own *bangsa*.

is always better and safer to marry within one's own *bangsa*, even if the man was poor, 'for what is the use of having a full belly if the heart is sad?'

Intermarriage with Arabs

The small Arab community numbered 2,591 in 1947 and had an even sex ratio: 1,308 males and 1,283 females. They were almost entirely concentrated in the urban areas, 90 per cent of them being returned in the Municipality. Many of them claimed descent from the Prophet, and as such used the title of *Sayed* for a man and *Sherifa* for a woman before their personal name: for instance, *Sayed* Ahmad, *Sherifa* Patimah. This descent, coupled with the fact that there were some very wealthy families among them, endowed the community as a whole with considerable prestige *vis-à-vis* the Malays. Arabs had founded and were managing several well-established Muslim charities[1] and religious schools. Moreover, some Arabs were emerging as political leaders, claiming to speak as representatives of the Colony's Muslim population, the large majority of whom were of course Malays.

There was some intermarriage between Arab men and Malay women, whereas the degree of intermarriage between Arab women and Malay men was practically nil. This was due to the fact that in cases where the woman was a *Sherifa* she was prohibited from marrying a non-*Sayed*, which in effect also meant a non-Arab since the Prophet's descendants are of course Arabs or of Arab origin.[2] The title of *Sayed* or *Sherifa* is passed on in the male line only, and marriage of a *Sayed* to a non-*Sherifa* is allowed. On the other hand, an Arab woman not of the line of the Prophet (i.e. not a *Sherifa*) still considered herself, and was also usually considered by the Malay community, as superior to any Malay by virtue of the country of origin of her ancestors.[3] Consequently, an Arab non-*Sherifa* was given by her parents to a Sayed or to a non-Sayed Arab. On the other hand, many Arab men took Malay women as wives, although their first marriage was usually arranged with an Arab woman. The Arabs practised polygyny, and the wealthier among them took Malay women as second or third wives. Here it must be stressed that immigration from Arabia was almost exclusively limited to males and that the so-called Arab women, and many of the Arab men, of Singapore are the offspring of Arab fathers and Malay mothers and usually cannot speak Arabic.

SOCIAL CONTROL: ADAT AND ISLAM

Adat

Peninsular Malays follow one or other of two distinct systems of customary

[1] See C. B. Buckley, *An Anecdotal History of Old Times in Singapore*, 2 vols., Singapore 1902, vol. 2, p. 564.

[2] S. Vesey-Fitzgerald in *Muhammadan Law*, London 1931, p. 55, states that 'All descendants of the Prophet (saiyyid, sharif) rank as pure Arabs'.

[3] Vesey-Fitzgerald, loc. cit., says that according to all schools of Islam 'a non-Arab is not an equal match for an Arab woman'.

law, the *adat pĕrpateh* and the *adat tĕmĕnggong*.[1] The former operates in a lineage system in which descent is traced through women. This system prevails in Minangkabau (Sumatra) and in many parts of Negri Sembilan in the Malay Peninsula. The Negri Sembilan settlers are descendants of emigrants from Minangkabau; some other Minangkabau emigrants are also settled in the Naning area of Malacca and there are some in Lukut in Johore. The *adat tĕmĕnggong* is associated with a bilateral system in which descent is traced through the father, but where no lineage organization exists. This *adat* (or custom) is followed by the rest of the Peninsular Malays.

Singapore Malays likewise follow *adat tĕmĕnggong* and here, therefore, we shall be concerned exclusively with it. In this context it is important to note that the overwhelming majority of Singapore Malays have never heard of the existence of the *adat pĕrpateh* and are not even familiar with the term *adat tĕmĕnggong*. They simply use the word *adat* when they want to refer to their own specific Malay customs, sometimes saying *adat orang Mĕlayu*, the custom of the Malay people. They themselves differentiate between traditional custom or *adat* and religious law or *hukum*.[2] They will say, for instance, that according to *hukum* or Muslim law there is no ban on marriage between the children of two brothers, but that according to *adat* such a union must be avoided. They also point out that Islam and *adat* disagree in the matter of inheritance, the former favouring males and the latter females; they add that, since women are the weaker sex and are usually incapable of earning a good income or of accumulating capital by their own effort, it is fair and wise that they should be generously treated in *adat*.

It is interesting to note that some local compilations of *adat tĕmĕnggong* contain specific references to, or applications of, Muslim law: the Malacca Laws, the Pahang Digest (sixteenth century), and the Ninety-Nine Laws of Perak compiled in the eighteenth century.[3]

Whereas in 1950 the *adat pĕrpateh* was recognized both by Malays and by the British administration as being a fairly definable system, *adat tĕmĕnggong* enjoyed no such status. In the Colony of Singapore there were two legal systems in force with regard to the Muslim population, English law and Islam. Apart from the fields of marriage, divorce and intestacy in inheritance—all of which were regulated according to Islam—Malays and other Muslims in the Colony were governed in all matters according to the English law in force in the Colony. As a result they could disinherit their wives and children by leaving a will to that effect, although this is

---

[1] For an interesting discussion on the origin and meaning of the two terms see P. E. de Josselin de Jong, *Minangkabau and Negri Sembilan: Socio-Political Structure in Indonesia*, Leiden 1951, pp. 168-72.

[2] The full term for religious law is *Hukum shara'*, but the second of these words is usually omitted by Malays.

[3] See R. J. Wilkinson, *Law, Part I*, in *Papers on Malay Subjects*, Kuala Lumpur, 1908. Also, R. Winstedt, op. cit., ch. 6.

strictly contrary to Islam which allows only one third of an estate to be willed away and enjoins, moreover, that this provision should be used for Muslim charities and organizations, and not to favour one heir against another. While some Singapore Arabs took advantage of the law to dispose of the whole of their property by will, wills were almost unknown among Malays who usually settled the matter of inheritance according to their *adat*.[1]

Islam

Malays of the Archipelago were peacefully converted to Islam in the fourteenth and fifteenth centuries by traders and missionaries from India and Sumatra. They are Sunnis and belong to the Shafi'i school of Islam which is generally followed in Egypt and Southern Arabia. Nearly every Malay village or district in Singapore has a mosque, and the chief official in charge of it is known as the *imam*. In popular speech the term *imam* is also used by Singapore Malays to describe a *kathi*; a *kathi* is an official (appointed by Government) empowered to register Muslim marriages and divorces.[2]

The five pillars of Islam are:
1. The doctrine of the Unity of God whose Divine Apostle is Mohammed.
2. The five daily prayers.
3. The annual fast during the month of Ramadan.
4. The pilgrimage to Mecca.
5. Annual payment of *zakat*, the religious tax or tithe.

1. Singapore Malays accept wholeheartedly the doctrine that there is only one God and that Mohammed is His Prophet.

2. Only a small proportion of the Malay population in the Colony, however, regularly prayed five times a day, or said they did so.

3. Again, only a small proportion fasted during the whole of the month of Ramadan. One popular practice was to fast only on the first and last few days of the month, and I came across a large number of persons who observed the fast only on the last day. In some States of the Peninsula Malays were prosecuted by government for not observing the fast; penalties consisting of fines or imprisonment, or both, were imposed on those found guilty. In the Colony, however, they were entirely at liberty to eat privately or publicly if they chose to do so.

4. The pilgrimage to Mecca is a very costly enterprise, but yields enormous prestige. On their return from Arabia, pilgrims are entitled to the term *Haji* (if a man) or *Haja* (if a woman) as a prefix to their name. Thus

---

[1] See below, pp. 40f.

[2] According to the Mohammedans Ordinance, Section 4, 1 (Chapter 57 of the 1936 edition of *The Laws of the Straits Settlements*, vol. 2), in force in the Colony in 1949 and 1950, 'The Governor may appoint any male Mohammedan of good character and position to be a Kathi.' *Kathi* have jurisdiction in a certain area or district, or for a particular 'nationality or sect'.

a man who was plain Omar *bin* Ahmad becomes on his return from Mecca *Haji* Omar *bin* Ahmad and usually wears a white cap or turban as a symbol of his status.[1] His children, in turn, are called *bin* (or *binti*) *Haji* Omar. Some Malays save money patiently for decades, or sell their possessions, in order to pay for the pilgrimage.[2] It is mainly members of the age-group 40-60 years who undertake the journey.

5. *Zakat* was rarely paid by Singapore Malays in 1949 and 1950. They paid *fitrah* voluntarily, however. This is another religious annual contribution, destined for the poor. Singapore Malays gave it to mosque officials, orphans and destitutes. In contrast to the Malay States, there was no legal machinery in the Colony to enforce the payment of either *zakat* or *fitrah*.

In 1949 and 1950 visitors to Singapore from Arab or Middle Eastern countries were struck by the comparative mildness of religious observance among the Malays. It is true that there was strict adherence to the taboo on pork, that the circumcision of boys was universal, that practically no living Malay was known to have abandoned Islam in favour of some other religion, that almost all boys and girls were formally taught to recite verses from the Koran and certain prayers, that marriages were solemnized by a *kathi*, divorces granted according to Muslim law, and that burials took place according to Muslim rites. On the other hand, many Malays did not refuse beer or other alcohol when it was offered; only a handful understood the meaning of the prayers which they recited parrot-fashion in Arabic; Koran tuition was extremely rudimentary and rarely were the religious teachers fully qualified for the job; attendance at mosques for Friday midday prayers was slight, even in the case of men who were free at that hour; and the general standard of knowledge of the most elementary principles and beliefs of Islam was very low. It was therefore not surprising that leadership or active committee membership of Muslim societies and associations in the Colony was largely Arab and Indian.

The immigrant Indonesians appeared to be generally more devout than the indigenous population in matters concerning the fast of Ramadan, regular daily prayers, and Friday midday prayers at mosques.

COMMUNITY AND LEADERSHIP

During the first months of field research I was faced with the fundamental problem of determining whether the Census category of the Colony known as 'Malays and Other Malaysians' was in fact little more than a Census category, or whether one could justifiably speak of them as a group in a sociological sense. In this context one of the most salient points about the

[1] On the other hand, some old men learned in religious matters, who have not made the pilgrimage, also affect a white cap.

[2] W. S. Blunt, writing of the early 1880's, said: 'For the moment the Malays stand rather apart from other pilgrims at the shrines. They boast no great school of theology or particular religious complexion; and as pilgrims they are held in rather low esteem from their penurious ways.' W. S. Blunt, *The Future of Islam*, London 1882, p. 33.

group was the lack of established leaders drawn from their ranks. There was a princely family living in a very large and neglected mansion known as the *Istana Kampong Glam*[1] in the centre of the town. Its members were descended from the Sultan Hussein who signed the treaties of 1819 and 1824 surrendering the island of Singapore to the East India Company. The descendants of Sultan Hussein used the title of *Tĕngku* (roughly equivalent to the terms 'Prince' and 'Princess') as a prefix to their first names. The title passes from father to child.[2] Not all the Singapore *tĕngku* lived in the Istana. There were four small houses in other areas of the Colony where other *tĕngku* resided.

Singapore *tĕngku* were impoverished; some of them were employed as semi-skilled workmen and junior clerks. The *tĕngku* were not active politically in the Colony: there was no *tĕngku* in either the Executive or the Legislative Council; *tĕngku* were not candidates at Municipal elections; they took no part in discussions in the Malay or English press on the administration of the Colony; they were not prominent members of Malay Associations. Singapore *tĕngku* were related by kinship to the Ruling Houses of some of the Malay States in the Peninsula and many alternated their residence between the Colony and these States. Unlike Malay society in the States of the Federation, Malay society in Singapore was devoid of its aristocratic leadership.

Attempts were being made, on the other hand, by Arabs and Indian Muslims, resident in Singapore, to assume leadership of the Colony's Malays by claiming to speak for them as Muslims. Here it must be noted that Malays were not treated by Government as a discrete sub-division of Singapore society except in so far as specialist provisions were made for them as Muslims. There were several voluntary Muslim associations in the Colony, but the leadership in them was almost entirely Arab and Indian. This was not only because Arabs and Indians were on the whole more devout Muslims than Malays, but also because many among them had reached positions of prestige through their wealth and occupation: there were several Arab and Indian lawyers, doctors, large-scale businessmen and landowners. In political discussions and in Government debates these men spoke as representatives of the Colony's Muslims, that is of the Malays as well as of the Arabs and Indians. Their authority to do so was not publicly contested by the Malay population. However, neither the Arabs nor the Indians had as yet completely assimilated themselves to the Malays. The latter referred to them specifically as *orang Arab* or *orang India*.[3] In the main link binding them together—Islam—the immigrant

---

[1] Lit., Kampong Glam Palace, Kampong Glam being the name of the district where the Istana was situated.

[2] The wife of a *tĕngku* or the adopted child of a *tĕngku* cannot acquire the title and is addressed as a commoner unless of course born a *tĕngku*.

[3] Before Indian independence, Indian immigrants were called *orang Bĕnggali*, *orang Tamil*, etc. In 1950 the term 'Pakistani' was not used to describe Muslim Indians resident in the Colony.

groups also showed a sign of differentiation: they went to an Arab and to an Indian *kathi*, respectively, for their marriage ceremonies and for divorce procedure. There were twelve *kathi* and one Chief *Kathi* in the Colony. *Kathi* were appointed by the Governor and their jurisdiction limited to the fields of Muslim marriage and divorce. They were not required to have gone through a course of formal specialized training in order to become eligible for the post.[1] The Malay population were aware of this and on the whole they did not consider their *kathi* as spiritual leaders, but as officials with special powers.

Since neither hereditary nobility nor religious office provided leaders in effect for the Malay population of Singapore, the Arab and Indian attempts at leadership became possible. There was closer contact between the Arabs and the Malays, however, than between the Indians and the Malays. Malays showed great deference to Arab residents, especially those descended from the Prophet. The latter were frequently addressed and referred to as *Těngku* by Malays, the term traditionally reserved for hereditary Malay nobles. In one very significant aspect, intermarriage, the relationship between Arabs and Malays could be compared to that between hereditary nobility and commoners: the rule of hypergamy was observed in such intermarriage, as we saw earlier. There was a further parallel between Arabs in the Colony and Malay noblemen in the Federation. Both took as their first wife a woman of equivalent status; an Arab man took an Arab woman and a Malay nobleman took a Malay noblewoman. These first marriages were usually family arrangements. Later, the Arab could, and often did, marry a Malay woman as a second or third wife, and the Malay nobleman a woman from the people.[2]

The Colony's Arabs followed a general pattern of living which was almost indistinguishable from that of the Malays. They spoke Malay in their homes, dressed like Malays, and they cooked and ate like Malays. They followed Malay rites and ceremonies at births and weddings. As was noted earlier, Singapore Arabs were frequently the offspring of Malay mothers and Arab fathers, and the Arab fathers were often themselves of similar mixed descent.

In Singapore in 1950, however, Arab-Indian leadership was not going totally unchallenged. From among the ranks of the more educated Malays

---

[1] The Muslim Advisory Board, a body consulted by Government on matters concerning Muslim law and practice, were advocating in 1950 more careful selection in the appointment of *kathi*, preferably through a system of examinations, to ensure an adequate knowledge of Muslim law.

[2] There was also intermarriage in the Federation between Arabs (especially *Sayed*) and the Malay nobility: it occurred between *Sayed* and Malay female *těngku*, however, rather than between *Sherifa* and Malay male *těngku*. The descendants of the Prophet still adhered to the old Arab rule that the only suitable husband for a *Sherifa* is a *Sayed*. After the Japanese Occupation, however, a few exceptions to this rule occurred and gave rise to much comment.

employed as schoolteachers, journalists, clerks, and Government officials, there were attempts at rivalry.

After the war, a young Malay lawyer resident in Singapore won considerable support from fellow-Malays in his campaign for organizing Malay religious and political associations. He had studied in England and spoke English fluently. He became a member of the Legislative Council and as such his statements carried a measure of authority. Both young and old Malays showed immense pride in him, and his name became known even in isolated rural areas. He made frequent public speeches, granted newspaper interviews, and for a time even toyed with the idea of founding a 'Malay Political Party' in the Colony. He gathered round him a group of ambitious Malays, many of whom were young men fired with a sincere and passionate zeal to better the status of their community. Thus it seemed that nascent leadership of Malays by Malays was emerging; but whether this leadership would work harmoniously with Arab-Indian leadership, or eventually supersede it, could not be determined in 1950.

COMMUNITY LIFE

In Malay villages in the rural areas of Singapore, the inhabitants formed a community in the sense that a village was a territorially compact group of people performing a wide range of functions. The villagers knew each other personally, being often related by birth or affinity among themselves. They had been born in the house built by their parents or grandparents, and would probably be buried in the village cemetery; their children went to the same school and were taught to read the Koran by the same religious teacher; the same local midwife delivered all the babies. On religious festivals the men assembled at the local mosque to pray. If the village well fell into disrepair every household contributed towards the cost of the necessary materials and the able-bodied men set to work on the job. When there was a death, every household contributed towards the expenses of the burial ceremonies.

The distinction was made between 'a child of the village' (*anak ini kampong*) and one who was 'not a child of this village' (*bukan anak ini kampong*) usually on the basis of the place of birth of the person concerned.[1] The position of the descendants of an old Tanjong couple may serve as an illustration. One of their daughters had married and settled in Tanjong and her children in turn became members of the village, *anak* Tanjong. One of their sons, on the other hand, had before the war married a girl from an islet off the coast, Pulau Damar, and made the islet his home. His children were born in Pulau Damar and brought up there; they were not *anak* Tanjong, but *anak* Pulau Damar. Another sister had married a man from a village in the State of Johore and settled there and her offspring

[1] Usually, because if a baby was born while his parents were only temporarily resident in a village, and they later moved away, the baby was said to belong not to the village of his birth, but to the permanent place of residence of the household.

in turn were not *anak* Tanjong. Thus the children of three full siblings claimed membership of three different localities. Both the brother and sister who had left Tanjong remained *anak* Tanjong and were strangers in their respective spouses' villages. There were countless similar instances in other areas of the Colony.

In some Singapore coastal kampongs there was a ritual performed every year or two, which was the most concrete expression of the fact that in these cases the village was conceived of as a separate entity. This was the ceremony known as *bĕla kampong*, fostering, protecting, the village. Its function was to cleanse the *kampong* of any evil ghosts or supernatural threats to the inhabitants' health and prosperity. I witnessed this ceremony in March 1950 in Tanjong. Every household contributed a dollar towards the expense, and nearly every person, man, woman, and child, helped with the preparations. The men built and carved a miniature boat; the women cooked sweetmeats of seven different varieties, dyed raw grains of rice in the colours of the rainbow and arranged them on trays in various shapes and representations. They also prepared a great deal of paper decorations. The children helped to run errands to the shops, to fetch water from the well, to borrow trays and cooking utensils from the houses of those who could spare them. Several villagers kept a vigil all night near the miniature boat now filled to capacity with the sweetmeats and other food offerings; and a live chicken, its legs tied together, was also placed in the boat. At dawn the next morning, the village magician, the *bomor*, set out with two men in his fishing boat after a procession of young men had gently lowered the miniature boat of offering inside the fishing boat. He sailed away for two hours, then abandoned the boat of offering to drift, and returned to Tanjong.

The whole of that day, from morning till dusk, the villagers were not allowed to dig the earth; to cut a leaf or a branch from any village tree or shrub; to draw water from the wells, or even from the newly-installed village water pipe. Parents carefully watched over their small children to see that they did not violate any of these taboos, for nothing must be torn away or drawn from the village. For three days, moreover (during that day and the following two days) the village remained taboo to all outsiders, whatever their religion or nationality, under penalty of a small token fine. It was also decided formally by the leaders of the village (the headman, the magician, and some of the more respected fishermen) that the next ceremony would take place exactly two years hence. The villagers explained to me that the ritual could never be dispensed with, or else disaster would soon fall upon the inhabitants. During the war they were evacuated to another area and they could not *bĕla kampong* there, simply because it was not their own *kampong* of Tanjong. 'What happened?' they asked rhetorically. Tanjong villagers died like flies, or contracted many diseases.[1] When

---

[1] During the Japanese occupation there was a shortage of food and of medical services. There were also frequent epidemics of malaria and typhoid fever.

the war was over and they returned to their native village, they held the *bĕla kampong* ceremony again, and were holding it regularly since, with the result—as everyone could see—that there had been few illnesses or deaths. The guardian spirits of the village were being properly propitiated.

In the urban areas of the Colony where there was a concentration of Malays, I knew of no comparable example where community feeling was as intense as in villages of the type of Tanjong. Although there was often a local mosque, a local vernacular school, and sometimes also one local midwife, the Malay inhabitants of any urban district did not appear to feel closely bound to each other, and certainly they rarely acted as a group. There were obvious reasons for this. Urban districts were not often delimited by visible boundaries which could compare with the bare patches of land surrounding a Malay village. There might be Chinese or Indians living in the next house, or in the next street. The Malay inhabitants themselves, at least the adults, were usually born in another district of the Colony and had rarely lived in the house they now occupied for more than a few years. As a rule, they did not own the house but rented it from a Chinese or from an Arab. They would move out if the head of the household changed his job and found it more convenient to live within closer proximity of his new place of work. In the villages, men sought jobs which were easily accessible to their homes. In the town they sought homes which were near the area in which they found employment.

One significant aspect of the lack of a strong community tie in urban districts was that whereas membership of a death-benefit association in a Malay village was limited to the inhabitants of that particular village, in the town these associations were based, not on common residence, but often on common occupation. Thus there were death-benefit associations for Malay drivers, for fitters, policemen, etc.

On the other hand, although community feeling was intense only in small villages and practically non-existent in urban and suburban areas, and although there were neither hereditary nor elected leaders acting specifically as representatives of Singapore Malays, yet that segment of the Colony's population was more than just a census category. One Malay identified another by certain explicit and implicit criteria. Malays are not a race in the strict sense of the term, but there was usually enough physical difference between them and other elements in the Colony's population to make them distinguishable on physical grounds. These physical characteristics were reinforced by peculiarities of dress, gait and posture. In addition there was language: Malay as spoken by the Malays among themselves was distinct from the varieties spoken by the local Chinese, the Indians, the Eurasians, and the Europeans. Apart from these immediately perceptible traits, Singapore Malays had many other points in common. They had rites and ceremonies connected with childbirth, circumcision, marriage and death which were peculiar to them not only as Muslims, but as Malays.

However, the most important point in this context was that Malays felt considerable in-group solidarity. This feeling found expression in their phrase *kita orang Mĕlayu* (we Malay people) which they used to refer to themselves as a discrete section of the Island's population. Singapore Malays attempted to form themselves into voluntary associations for charitable purposes and for economic co-operation. Malay women of the Colony started organizations for the purposes of helping destitute mothers and widows and of providing financial help for the sick. The rules of these organizations specifically stated that recipients of the services must be Malays resident in the Colony.

The majority of Malay charitable associations were of recent (post-war) origin. They had not accumulated much capital by 1950; membership fluctuated; suitable premises were not always available; and committees did not always work smoothly. However, their formation was an undeniable attempt by Singapore Malays to give concrete expression to the fact that they considered themselves to be one unitary body.

2

Kinship

THE kinship system of Singapore Malays is bilateral, or cognatic, in the sense that equal or almost equal importance is attached to kin on the father's and on the mother's side. There are no different sets of kinship terms used (either in address or reference) for paternal and maternal relatives. For instance, *pak saudara* refers to the brother of one's father as well as to that of one's mother, and by extension to the husband of either parent's sister. Similarly, one refers to one's parallel cousin (whether paternal or maternal), as well as to one's cross-cousin, as *sa-pupu*. If elucidation is sought, the question asked is, 'In what way is so-and-so your *pak saudara* (or your *sa-pupu*)? On your father's side, or on your mother's side? *Sa-bĕlah bapa kah, sa-bĕlah ĕmak?*'

Singapore Malays trace descent from the father, but have no family surnames. If a couple, Ahmad and Puteh, have a son Osman, he will be called Osman *bin* Ahmad (*bin* = son of). If they have a daughter Ramla, she will be Ramla *binti* (daughter of) Ahmad. Osman's son Ali in turn will be Ali *bin* Osman. This is the Islamic system of naming.[1] Records of births and deaths in a family are not normally kept, the names of the dead do not always appear on tombstones, and so it is rare for a Malay to know the name of a great-grandparent. Moreover, on account of the naming system, the names of grandfathers rather than of grandmothers tend to be remembered.

While nominally descent is traced from father to child, and while for certain specific purposes, also in accordance with Islam, certain paternal relatives are vested with special rights and duties, nevertheless any individual in the society regards himself as equally related to the kin of his father and his mother. The result is that apart from unmarried full siblings any two persons have a different range of kindred.

Singapore Malays use colloquially one term only when they wish to refer to one or more members of the total group of their kindred, the word *saudara*. (*Saudara* is also often used to refer specifically to the group of one's siblings.) This term is applied to relatives by blood, by adoption (specifically *saudara angkat*), and sometimes with the addition of the term

---

[1] Islam, however, does not forbid the additional use of surnames or of tribal names. Both are found in Arabia.

ipar to affines, *saudara ipar*. People who are not one's *saudara* are *orang lain*.[1] In contrast to some parts of the Malay Peninsula the word *waris* is not used in Singapore to describe everyone with whom consanguineous connection can be traced. *Waris* appears, rather, to apply exclusively to one's heirs or potential heirs, and this usage of course coincides with the actual Arabic meaning of the word.

Singapore Malays themselves distinguish between *saudara děkat* (close relatives) and *saudara jauh* (distant relatives). *Saudara děkat* include one's ancestors and direct descendants; one's siblings and their children; and the siblings of one's parents and their children. Second cousins, the grand-children of one's siblings, the siblings of one's grandparents, first cousins of one's parents, and children of one's first cousins are also frequently considered *děkat*; but on the other hand if a Malay wishes to be partly dissociated from such a kinsman he states, 'So-and-so is not really a *saudara děkat* of mine; he is *děkat* to my mother [or father] but with me he is already *sikit jauh*, a little distant.' Or else, 'Our parents are *děkat*, true, but we the children are not so *děkat*, *ta' běrapa děkat*.'

Saudara jauh are third cousins, second cousins of one's parents, children of one's second cousins, and anybody more distantly related.

The *saudara jauh* of one's own *saudara děkat* are *orang lain*. Moreover, many Singapore Malays consider as *orang lain* the *saudara děkat* of their own *saudara děkat*.

Apart from the fact that kin groups are not mutually exclusive, there is also an absence of a clear-cut line beyond which one can say that such-and-such a person is not recognized as a *saudara*. Theoretically, fourth and fifth cousins can claim to be *saudara*, but no term is ordinarily used for such a relationship and it appears that such cousins usually merge into the group of *orang lain*.

So far I have been speaking of consanguineous kin. The other two categories are those relating to adoptive and to affinal kin. If an individual is fully and permanently adopted from infancy, the range of his *saudara* and their division into *děkat* and *jauh* is the same as if he had been actually begotten by his adoptive parents.

The position of affines, however, is not so clearly definable. There is no specific term in general use for affines, although the expression *saudara ipar* is heard in this context. The fact that the relationship is entirely based on a particular marriage, that the rate of divorce is extremely high, and that if this marriage is dissolved the affinal link is automatically severed, may account for the lack of precision in labelling those relatives.[2] Although

---

[1] The expression *orang lain* is used by Malays in two contexts. It is a general label applied to any individual who is a complete stranger, such as a newcomer to a village. It is also used specifically to refer to a person with whom no kinship link is traced.

[2] The affinal link is considerably attenuated if the individual who is the *trait-d'union* between two affines dies. For instance, when a woman's husband dies, her

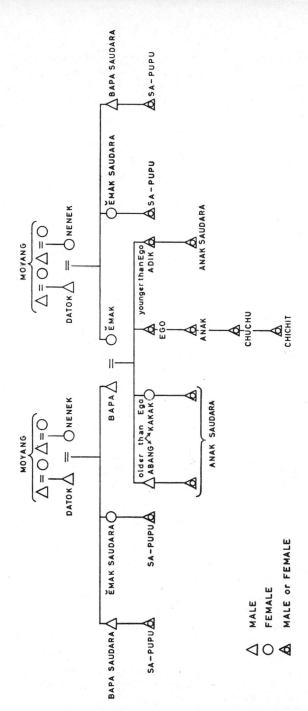

SAUDARA DĚKAT

Terms of Reference

c

many informants stated that some affines (such as the parents and siblings of one's spouse and the spouses of one's children and of one's siblings) are *saudara děkat*, the majority of Singapore Malays maintain that all affinal relatives are *orang lain*, however close the degree of affinity. They use the term *saudara*, or more commonly the expression *bukan orang lain*, to refer to consanguineous relatives and to persons taken from infancy in full adoption. *Saudara ipar*, they add, is a term serving to differentiate affines from among the mass of complete strangers. It is interesting that whereas a consanguineous kinsman might be referred to simply as one's *saudara* (without specifying the degree of the relationship), an affine is usually referred to specifically as being one's *anak měnantu* (son or daughter-in-law), *mak měrtua* (mother-in-law), *biras* (husband of wife's sister), etc.

Kinship Terminology

Malays, in common with many other peoples, use a classificatory type of kinship terminology. Such a terminology makes it possible to distinguish 'a few categories of relationship under which a very large number of near and distant relatives can be included'.[1] The categories are usually based on the division into generations.

CONSANGUINEOUS KIN

Within the elementary family the following is the terminology used:

	Reference	Address
Father	Bapa	Bapa (more commonly Pak)
Mother	Ěmak	Ěmak (,, ,, Mak)
Child or children	Anak	Name of child
Son or sons	Anak laki-laki	,, ,, ,,
Daughter or daughters	Anak pěrěmpuan	,, ,, ,,
Older brother	Abang	Name, or Abang + name
Older sister	Kakak	Name, or Kak + name
Younger brother or sister	Adik	Name

The same terms are normally used between half-siblings as between full siblings, although other expressions exist for purposes of differentiation: siblings born of the same father but of different mothers are *saudara bětul* (*bětul* means real, true), whereas siblings born of the same mother but of different fathers are *saudara anjing* (*anjing* means dog). These are terms of reference only.

In polite speech Malays refer to, and sometimes address, their father as *ayah* and their mother as *ibu*.

When we come to consanguineous kin outside the elementary family the following terms apply, and there is no differentiation in any instance between people related to one on the father's and on the mother's side:

husband's siblings are not considered as closely related to her as they were during her husband's lifetime. Many Singapore Malays even assert that the widow and her husband's siblings then become strangers.

[1] A. R. Radcliffe-Brown, *Structure and Function in Primitive Society*, 1952, p. 67.

	Reference	*Address*
Grandfather	Datok	Datok or Tok
Grandmother	Nenek (also Datok)	Nenek, Nek (also Datok and Tok)
Grandson or granddaughter	Chuchu	Name
Great-grandchild	Chichit	Name
Great-grandfather	Moyang	Datok or Tok
Great-grandmother	Moyang	Nenek, nek, also Datok, Tok
Father's or mother's brother	Bapa saudara	Pak long or Pak chik
Father's or mother's sister	Ĕmak saudara	Mak long or Mak chik
Sibling's child, male or female	Anak saudara	Name
First cousin (male or female parallel, or cross-cousin)	Sa-pupu	
If first cousin is		
older and a male	Abang sa-pupu	Abang + name
older and a female	Kakak sa-pupu	Kak + name
younger, male or female	Adik sa-pupu	Name
Father's or mother's first cousin (male)	Bapa saudara sa-pupu	As for father's or mother's brother
Father's or mother's first cousin (female)	Ĕmak saudara sa-pupu	As for father's or mother's sister
Child of one's first-cousin	Anak saudara sa-pupu	Name
Grandfather's or grandmother's brother	Datok saudara	Datok or Tok
Grandfather's or grandmother's sister	Nenek saudara	As for grandmother
Grandchild of brother or sister	Chuchu saudara	Name
Second cousin	Dua-pupu	As for first cousin
Third cousin	Tiga-pupu	As for first cousin

In the terms of address for the siblings of one's parents the words *long* and *chik* have been given. *Long* is short for *sulong*, which means first-born, *chik* is short for *kĕchik*, meaning little or small. Therefore *pak long* or *mak long* is often used when addressing a *pak saudara* or *mak saudara* if he or she is an older sibling of one's parent, even though not the eldest of the parent's group of siblings; and *pak chik* or *mak chik* if he or she is a younger sibling. These are the most frequent terms of address used in such situations. Other terms exist which are sometimes, though rarely, used in Singapore, such as *mak ngah* (when the *mak saudara* is younger than one's parent but is intermediate in the order of birth of all her siblings—*ngah* is short for *tĕngah* meaning half or middle) and *mak anjang* when the woman is still younger than her sibling who is addressed as *mak ngah*. *Mutatis mutandis* the same applies to the terms *pak ngah* and *pak anjang*. In this context it is worth pointing out that parents do not use the terms *anak ngah*, *anjang*, or *chik*, when referring to their children, although they do say *anak sulong* to refer to their first-born. They also use the term *anak bungsu* to refer to the youngest born child.

The most common usage in Singapore for the purpose of stating the order of birth of siblings is to employ numbers. *Numur* is the Malay version of the English word 'number'. Thus the first child is called *anak numur satu*, the second *anak numur dua*, the third *anak numur tiga*, the fourth *anak numur ĕmpat*, and so on. The numbers apply strictly to the order of birth, and if intermediate children have died the younger ones do not change their number. For instance, if a couple have only three surviving children they may refer to the youngest alive as *anak numur tujoh (tujoh = 7)*; they then add that their children numbers one, three, five and six, are dead or were still-born.

Where first cousins are concerned, there is a Javanese variation in the terminology. The Javanese immigrants refer to and address *sa-pupu* as *abang*, *kakak*, or *adik* not according to the respective ages of the *sa-pupu* concerned, but following the order of birth of the parents.[1] The following diagram helps to illustrate this usage:

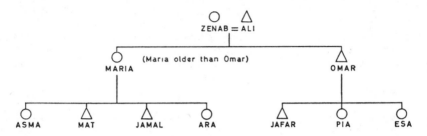

All three children of Omar consider themselves as the *adik sa-pupu* of Asma, Mat, Jamal, and Ara, even if in point of fact they are older in years, because their *mak saudara* Maria is older than their father Omar. Similarly Maria's sons will refer to themselves as the *abang sa-pupu*, and her daughters as the *kakak sa-pupu*, of Jafar, Pia, and Esa. In other words, for the purposes of kinship terminology, children inherit the age status of their parent in this context. Thus Ara aged 18 years will be referred to, and addressed, by her first-cousin Jafar, aged 27 years, as *kakak*.

From the list of kinship terms given on the preceding pages it has become apparent that the words that occur most frequently are *bapa*, *ĕmak*, *anak*, *abang*, *kakak*, and *adik*. They are used to express kinship relations of the first order; and compounded with the word *saudara* they serve to express most of the other orders of consanguineous relationship. It is necessary here to stress that Malays, when asked how a person is related to them, rarely give the full title which will indicate the precise relationship. Thus

[1] cf. H. Subandrio, *Javanese Peasant life. Villages in East Java*, Unpublished thesis submitted for the Academic Post-Graduate Diploma in Anthropology, University of London, May, 1951, pp. 55-6. 'When the family relationship is clear, the age is of no importance in addressing relatives. One calls every male person of senior relative's group "Kakang" or "Mas" regardless of age.'

when speaking of an older first cousin they often just say *abang* or *kakak*; only when one insists, *abang bĕtul?* or *kakak bĕtul?* do they specify *abang sa-pupu* or *kakak sa-pupu*. If the relationship is more distant, such as that between second or third cousins and if, as often happens, they are not sure which of the two it is, they often use the term *abang saudara* or *kakak saudara*. Similarly, they may always have referred to an older woman in their group of kindred as *mak saudara* without knowing what the exact relationship was; if one should ask them what type of *mak saudara* the woman was to them, the answer is in case she is not a *mak saudara bĕtul*: 'I don't know exactly, all I do know is that she is *pangkat mak saudara sama saya*, of the status (*pangkat*) of *mak saudara vis-à-vis* myself.' This use of the term *pangkat* to differentiate between generations is very common, particularly when the exact link is not known. For instance a woman once said to me: 'Che' Liyah is my *nenek saudara*. I do not know how we are related, but I know that my mother referred to her as her *mak saudara*, therefore with regard to me Che' Liyah must be *pangkat nenek* (of the status of a grandmother) since she was *pangkat ĕmak* to my mother.'[1]

AFFINAL KIN

	Reference	Address
Wife	Bini (politely istĕri)	Name
Husband	Laki (politely suami)	Name, or politely Abang
Father-in-law	Bapa mĕrtua	Bapa or Pak
Mother-in-law	Ĕmak mĕrtua	Ĕmak or Mak
Son-in-law or daughter-in-law	Anak mĕnantu	Name
Stepfather	Bapa tiri	Bapa or Pak
Stepmother	Ĕmak tiri	Ĕmak or Mak
Stepchild	Anak tiri	Name
Older stepbrother	Abang tiri	Name, or Abang + name
Older stepsister	Kakak tiri	Name, or Kak + name
Younger stepbrother or younger stepsister	Adik tiri	Name
Spouse's sibling	Ipar	As for own sibling

Husbands of two sisters are *biras* to each other and will themselves use this term of reference; they address each other as *abang* or *adik* plus name, or if they are friendly and the difference in their ages is small they may simply address each other by name. There is no corresponding term for the wives of two brothers, the word *ipar* being used in this context. Two sets of parents of a married couple are *besan* to each other. They address each other either as strangers would, e.g. *Che'* plus name, or else *abang kakak*, or *adik*, according to sex and age. It is rare in Singapore for a *besan*

[1] Che', short for Inche', is a polite prefix to a Malay man's or woman's name. It is roughly equivalent to Mr, Mrs, or Miss.

to address his or her *besan* as *Tok besan*, a practice apparently more common in the Federation of Malaya.

Co-wives refer to each other as *madu* and address each other as *kakak*, or *kak* plus name and *adik* plus name according to their age. The children of the newer wife refer to the father's older wife as *ĕmak tiri*, or stepmother, whereas those of the older wife refer to their father's newer wife as *ĕmak muda* (young mother). The wives themselves refer to each other's children by the common husband as *anak tiri* (stepchildren) and the children of the different wives use among themselves the terms for address given above for siblings.

Generally speaking, when the relationship is close, one does not always distinguish in terms of address or of reference between consanguineous relatives and the spouses of these relatives. Thus the husband of one's *mak saudara* is referred to as *bapa saudara* and addressed as *pak long* or *pak chik*; similarly the wife of one's *sa-pupu* is referred to and addressed in the same way as one's own female *sa-pupu* would be. This must not, of course, be taken to mean that the relationship is felt to be as close, but only that the terms are courtesy terms—for as soon as the union is dissolved by divorce (and sometimes even by death) the persons become strangers again, *orang lain*. Also should one ask further, 'Is so-and-so your *bapa saudara bĕtul?*', the answer is, 'Not *bĕtul*, but he is married to my *mak saudara* and so he has become my *bapa saudara, jadi bapa saudara*.'

At marriage, a person acquires a kinship status equivalent to that of his or her spouse *vis-à-vis* the spouse's kinsmen. This fact may lead to an embarrassing situation, involving a rearrangement of attitudes and of terms of address and of reference. Here is an instance of a case I observed in 1949.

Puteh was a young girl of nineteen, and her friend Asma who was of the same age used to address her by name. Asma had married Mat, the son of a widower, a year earlier. Mat's father then arranged to marry Puteh and the latter therefore became the stepmother of Asma's husband. After the wedding, Asma could no longer address Puteh by name, but called herself self-consciously *Mak* Puteh (Mother Puteh) and referred to her in the same way. The relationship between the two young women also became more formal, and they appeared ill at ease when in each other's company.

ADOPTIVE KIN

Adoption is very widespread among Malays. 16 of the 48 households in Tanjong included adopted children. Full adoption gives an individual the status of a consanguineous relative in the new kin group. The person adopted refers to all the *saudara* of his adoptive parents as an 'own child' would; conversely, they address and refer to him as if he had actually been born into their own group. Thus the same terminology as is used among blood kindred occurs in such a situation. The term for an adopted child is *anak angkat*, but it is rare for adoptive parents normally to refer to the child as their *anak angkat*: they simply say *anak*, child, as they would if it were their own child.

Malays themselves use no special terms to differentiate between full and partial adoption. Partial adoption takes place when a child lives for several years with foster-parents; or when a Malay arrives in a new district where he has no relatives and some older person befriends him and becomes known as his adoptive parent; or if a child who is very ill is formally adopted in an attempt to cure it while in fact it continues to live with its real parents. The range of relationship created by this type of adoption is limited. It applies as between the person so adopted and the adoptive parent, with a possible extension to the spouse and children of the adoptive person, but no further.

Sometimes people who are not related to each other in any manner become close friends, and after the friendship has endured for some years one may refer to the other and perhaps also to the latter's very close kin as *saudara angkat*. Malays do not expect to find great intimacy outside the kin group, and when it does occur seem to wish to justify it by using kinship terms. For example a Malay village *imam* (mosque official) and his wife referred in conversation to a middle-aged couple of Boyanese rubber-tappers as their *saudara angkat*. When I asked how the relationship had started the *imam*'s wife explained to me:

'Some years ago my only daughter was very ill with beri-beri and we all thought she would die. This Boyanese man, whom we knew because he lives about two miles away and comes often to pray at our village mosque, then behaved with great kindness. He got a *bomor* from far away to come to attend to her, and was of very great help to us. He acted as my own relatives would, *macham saudara saya*, and since then has always been ready to be of service to us. His wife is also a very good woman, quiet, clean, and well-mannered. So we have become great friends, often visit each other, and do not hesitate to ask for and give help. Really one's own *saudara* could not be more obliging or sincere than those Boyanese have been to me, and so even though they are of a different 'race' (*sunggoh lain bangsa*) I consider them as my *saudara*, as my *saudara angkat*.'

In this case, however, the Malay couple addressed the Boyanese and his wife as *Che'* plus name; and they in turn were similarly addressed by the Boyanese couple. The latter also referred to the *imam* and his wife as their *saudara angkat*. As in the case of partial adoption, the *saudara angkat* relationship was restricted to the persons immediately involved: even the *imam*'s daughter, who had had beri-beri and recovered, as she believed, thanks to the rubber-tappers, did not refer to the Boyanese as her *saudara angkat*, nor did they to her.

SELECTION WITHIN THE GROUP OF KINDRED

Within the group of kindred a Malay frequently associates more closely with some members than with others, irrespective of the closeness or remoteness of the actual kinship link. The factors making for such selection are varied, and here I consider those which seem most relevant.

Paternal and Maternal Kin

Singapore Malays usually say that the kin of one's father are *lagi kuat* (lit. 'stronger') than the kin of one's mother. They point out that only a father or a paternal kinsman can act as *wali* (guardian) to give a girl away in marriage. This situation is regularly mentioned in any discussion on the necessity for keeping on good terms with paternal kin.

I found a tendency among my female informants to attach manliness to paternal relatives. For instance, a common argument in 'explanation' of the statement that paternal relatives enjoyed a status superior to that of maternal relatives was that men are stronger physically, are trained to earn wages, that they support the household, and that in some religious ceremonies such as a wedding or a burial ten women cannot take the place of one man at prayers. 'What do we women matter? We can only cook and keep house. A man is more capable and therefore the father's kinsmen are more important than the mother's.'

In practice, one finds that Malays visit their maternal relatives and go to them for advice and help more frequently than they do their paternal kin, provided of course that both sets live within roughly similar degrees of geographical accessibility. On ceremonial occasions, such as births, circumcisions, weddings, and funerals, both parties are invited and come to attend; but maternal relatives tend to offer more help with the cooking, sewing, and other arrangements. One of the chief reasons for this obvious preference in fact for the *saudara* of one's mother is that when she has a home of her own she tends to take her young children to visit and to stay with her own kinsmen more often than with her husband's kinsmen, and therefore the children become more familiar with their maternal kin. Another factor is the bias towards matrilocality both in the sense of residence in the same household as that of the wife's parents and of independent residence in the native village or district of the wife. Furthermore, a Malay woman prefers to go to the house of her sister rather than to that of her brother, of her mother's sister rather than to that of her mother's brother. She and her children spend more time in the company of the woman of the house than in that of the male host, and naturally she is more at ease if her hostess is her own kinswoman. Consequently one frequently hears the statement that *sa-pupu* who are the children of two sisters feel much closer to each other, like real siblings, *macham adik běradik bětul*, than *sa-pupu* who are the children of brother and sister or of two brothers. This, it is explained, is because they met constantly as children. (The closeness of the relationship, however, does not give rise to any traditional ban on marriage between the children of two sisters.) In this context it is also important to remember that Malay marriage unions are not very stable, and that since it is the practice for the children of a dissolved union to follow their mother, they will tend to see almost exclusively their maternal relatives. Where attitudes to paternal and maternal kinsmen are concerned, therefore, there is clearly a conflict between formal ideology (which is closely bound up with Islam) and practice.

In spite of what has just been said, it would be wrong to assume that the line between maternal and paternal kin can always be clearly demarcated. Often, husband and wife have common consanguineous kin; children of the union, therefore, will have kinsmen to whom they are related through both their father and their mother. This situation is common on account of the marked preference among Malays for a marriage partner who is already a kinsman. However, although paternal and maternal kin do not often form two distinct groups, the individuals who stand in exactly the same degree of proximity to both a husband and a wife are few in number. Marriages between first cousins do occur, and in such cases, of course, husband and wife have one pair of grandparents in common, and may have also common *pak saudara, mak saudara* and *sa-pupu*.

However, the majority of marriages between kin are based on a more remote degree of kinship than the link between first cousins. In such cases, not only is the total range of common relatives smaller, but also few of those relatives stand in an equal relationship to the husband and to the wife. Take the situation when *dua-pupu*, R and S, marry. T is the maternal uncle, or *pak saudara*, of the wife, but he is only the husband's *pak saudara sa-pupu*, his mother's first cousin. T is considered to be primarily the

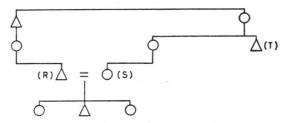

wife's *saudara* and in any serious quarrel between the couple he is expected to protect her interests. The three children of the pair consider T as a maternal kinsman; the closer link takes precedence over the more remote link. In this way, kinsmen with an unequal claim to the two groups are classified specifically as maternal relatives or as paternal relatives. This tendency makes for an easier demarcation of the groups by reducing the existing overlap between maternal and paternal kinsmen.

Geographical Nearness is very important, as Singapore Malays do not like to travel far afield and even full siblings may not exchange visits more frequently than three or four times a year if they live fifteen miles apart. On the other hand, siblings living in the same locality go to one another's homes several times a week.

Similarity of Income and Social Prestige in Malay as in Western society
helps to bring relatives closer together. Poor relations never tire of com-
plaining about being snubbed by their more prosperous *saudara*, while
the latter usually take meticulous care to be civil and pleasant to their less
fortunate kindred precisely because they worry lest they be accused of
haughty behaviour.

Friendship. A purely personal element is often responsible for drawing
individual relatives closer together. As a rule this occurs when the persons
concerned are of the same age and went to school together, or simply
when they enjoy each other's company. An added incentive is trust in
each other's discretion; one of the highest forms of praise in describing a
person's attributes is the statement *Dia ta' ada mulut* (he or she has no
mouth, i.e. does not gossip or tell tales). These friendships are between
relatives of the same sex, for it is not considered proper that boys and girls
who are past the age of childhood should play, or remain alone, together.

EMOTIONAL RELATIONSHIPS

The relationship between a Malay woman and her children is extremely
close and intense. We are familiar in Western society with the strong
attachment between a mother and her child, especially when it is not yet
in its teens; in our society, however, great value is set upon training the
young child as early as possible to become self-reliant and he is encouraged
to bear bravely a separation from his mother for a short or long period. In
Malay society a young child—especially a girl—would be considered unnatural if it did not at such a separation show great distress, loss of appetite,
and general fretfulness.

When adolescence is reached boys go out to work, have greater freedom
of movement, and begin to be interested in other women. Their sisters,
on the other hand, stay at home more than ever at that age and are in
constant contact with their mother who teaches them to cook, sew, mend,
and generally keep house. Even after they marry and have children of their
own in an independent household, women say they pine for their mother
if away from her for more than a few weeks.

Malay children are weaned fairly late, often not until two years old. I
saw a few children of four and five still coming once or twice a day to be
suckled. In such cases the child is usually the youngest, for the strain of
feeding two children simultaneously is said to be too great for a woman.
Although mothers complain about the difficulty of weaning a child, in
some instances it is they themselves who are not eager to put an end to
the suckling. One of my neighbours used to tell everybody that she found
it impossible to wean her daughter, aged two and a half years. She claimed
she had tried everything, including putting pepper and other sharp spices
on the breasts, but to no avail. On several occasions when she was not
aware I was watching her, however, I saw her take the girl in her arms
and attempt to suckle her. The child might be playing, or walking about

unconcernedly, and the mother would suddenly snatch her half playfully and place her breast in the child's mouth. Sometimes the girl would cry and free herself, at others she would happily nestle in her mother's arms and be suckled.

Close physical contact between mother and child also occurs in the sleeping situation. Children up to the age of five or six years sleep in very close proximity to their mother, often on the same mat, and the woman may take them in her arms during the night, and wake up to comfort them if they have a nightmare.

Both fathers and mothers rarely refuse to give their small children any form of food asked for, even if they know that the child will not be able to digest it. As the father is away from home most of the day, it is naturally to his mother that a child most often makes his requests for snacks or for anything in the kitchen. It is recognized that children's whims are often irresistible and that little boys and girls cannot understand that the cake or unripe fruit they want might upset them. This type of satisfaction is therefore rarely refused, and mothers occasionally go without a meal to spend the money on chocolates or boiled sweets for their small children.

When children are about six or seven years old, physical caresses get rarer but maternal affection is demonstrated in other ways, such as indulging their desire for special dishes or for new clothes.

Maternal feelings are fostered in a girl at a very early age. When she is seven or eight, she acts as a mother to her younger siblings, helps feed them, takes them out for a walk, changes their clothes when they get dirty or wet, and watches over them with great solicitude as they play with other babies. It is less common for a boy to look after his younger siblings. If a girl has no younger brothers or sisters, neighbours or close kinsmen often ask her to look after their small child during the day, while they are busy.

To be surrounded by members of his family helps to give a Malay a sense of security. If a man is out of work, if he is ill, if he is unhappy in his conjugal life, he can usually rely upon his parents or other close kin to help him with money, food, or care and attention, or advice. When a woman is in childbirth, or when her baby is ill, or when her husband ill-treats her, she can rely upon her parents or siblings or other close kin to look after her and her child, or to defend her. But apart from such crises there is the very real need for the constant presence of people whom one has known from childhood as *saudara*. A Singapore Malay seems to have a particular dread of solitude, of being *satu orang* (which literally means 'one person' and usually implies living alone), and even though he or she may live in a house with several people will still tend to feel alone if not related by kinship to any of them. A person who has no *saudara děkat* living, or whose *saudara děkat* reside several hours' journey away, is considered an object of pity however healthy and wealthy he may be; for he must feel so lonely, and should he suddenly fall ill he could depend implicitly on nobody to nurse him.

On one occasion a senior United Nations consultant came to visit me in Tanjong. I took her round the village, and we were invited into one of the homes. The villagers asked many personal questions, and in the end commented with deep sympathy, 'Poor lady. So she always lives alone, no parents, no husband, no children. How hard.' I explained that she had a very interesting job, travelled a great deal, and earned a large salary, but they were not impressed. 'Yes, yes, but she is still *satu orang*. Poor woman.'

Having a large group of kinsmen is a great asset, but the greatest of all is to have both parents alive. Married people with homes of their own feel the death of a parent as a grave loss and deprivation and look with great envy upon their friends who still have both parents. One common exclamation is *untong* (how profitable!, lit. profit) when it is learnt that an adult has both parents alive. At a large gathering of women at a feast, one of the guests asked another whether her father and mother were in good health. She replied that they were indeed, as was her old grandmother. When she heard this, a Malay woman of forty whose daughter was engaged to be married, exclaimed: 'How lucky this lady is! How I wish my own mother and grandmother were still alive, I would have such an easy time then!' I enquired how, and she explained: 'Well, because then I would be spoilt by them, and made a fuss of—*boleh manja sama dia!*'

Orphaned children are particular objects of pity, especially when they are doubly orphaned. This is so regardless of the fact that they may be tenderly cared for by relatives with a comfortable home. I remember how surprised I was one *hari raya* (the Malay festival occurring at the end of the fasting month, when people go visiting in their best clothes) at hearing several villagers remark about a pretty and very well dressed little girl who was eating sweets: 'Poor child, she is a full orphan; she has no father and no mother; it is good to give alms to such a child upon *hari raya*; she is a deserving case.' I commented that the girl seemed very well fed and looked after. 'Yes, her *mak saudara* who has no children and is quite prosperous has adopted her since she became orphaned, and she spoils her a great deal. Still, the child is an orphan, and we give her charity on that account; we give this money to her, not to her adoptive mother.'

That same day I was also informed that a wealthy neighbour had given two new suits of clothes on the occasion of *hari raya* to a small boy who also had been doubly orphaned but who for the last few years had been living in the comfortable home of the *kathi* as an adopted child. He was well fed and always neatly dressed. On the other hand, children of poor homes who walk about dressed in rags and do not always eat their fill do not attract so much pity if they have a father and a mother; and they do not have a prior claim to charity.

It is difficult to ascertain how much of this attitude is the result of indigenous Malay practice and how much it has been affected by Muslim precepts. Islam lays great stress on the need to protect the interests of orphans and on the duty of the more prosperous members of the community to shelter and care for such children.

The ties between a Malay and his kinsmen are severed only by death. He may have been given away in adoption in childhood, he may have quarrelled with his parents and left his home village for many years, but he still claims to be a member of the kin group, and they still claim him as belonging to them. For instance, should his real father be dying, one of his relatives will usually come to fetch him so that he can attend the funeral. When parents are angry with their children they often threaten to disown them, a threat which frightens younger people but does not usually have much effect upon more mature ones. I was told once by a girl who was in great distress because her relatives disapproved strongly of her suitor and had threatened to disown her if she saw him again: 'But he says that those are empty words, and perhaps he is right. He says that not even a tiger disowns its own young; they will be angry with me for a while but then we will make it up; it is like water which continues to run even though you put a knife through the flow.'[1] Eventually the couple were married without much ceremony—they forced the issue by having pre-marital relations—and after the lapse of a token period of estrangement between the girl and her close relatives, peace was made. The older sister with whom she had been living up to the time of her wedding made her gifts of a mattress, clothes, saucepans and other objects to help her set up a new household.

Serious injuries which, if they were caused by strangers, would create bitter and lasting enmity, are forgiven if they have occurred between *saudara děkat*. In Tanjong, a young girl discovered some months after her marriage that her husband was betraying her with her older sister who lived in the same household. The position was made worse by the fact that both women were pregnant simultaneously by him. There were loud and angry scenes; the wife was naturally incensed and cursed her sister bitterly. It was agreed that she would be divorced immediately and that the guilty pair would get married. The latter then went to live in the village of the husband while the younger woman continued to stay with her parents. Within a few months, however, the two sisters were again on speaking terms. There was general approval that the period of estrangement was of short duration, people commenting: 'Whatever happened, they are after all sisters; you cannot break that tie.'

ECONOMIC RELATIONS

1. *Ownership of Property*

Apart from personalia, the property of Singapore Malays usually con-

---

[1] C. C. Brown in *Malay Sayings*, London 1951, p. 126, quotes in the context of 'Kith and Kin' the saying *ayer di-chěnchang tidak putus* which he translates as 'slashed water is never severed'.

sisted of land, houses, furniture, gold jewelry, and tools of trade. Bank accounts or large savings in cash were rare. In parts of the Malaysian world some forms of property are *harta pusaka* (*pĕsaka*), that is to say ancestral property, which cannot be disposed of save in exceptional circumstances regulated by custom and usually also by law. *Harta pusaka* is found in the matrilineal areas of the Malay Peninsula and of Sumatra, among the Minangkabau. It is also found in Sarawak, among the Melanau[1] and among the Iban or Sea Dayak.[2] In Singapore, however, there appears to be no *harta pusaka* in the sense of inalienable ancestral property, although of course there is inherited property.

Land. Only a few hundred Singapore Malays owned land, usually orchard land, which they tended and which supplied them with a regular income; large landowners were unknown. The common pattern was for rural residents to own the plot of land on which their house was built, and an adjacent small strip of a few square feet with an odd banana or coconut tree. Sometimes, as in Tanjong, householders owned in addition a few fruit trees in a patch of orchard land lying outside the inhabited area of the village. These trees, however, did not give enough fruit for the needs of the owner, who had to supplement the yield with purchases from the local shopkeeper. Unlike the rural Chinese, who were busily engaged in market gardening and poultry and pig rearing, and who made use of the tiniest patch of land, Singapore Malays showed little interest in cultivation and very few of them troubled to keep more than two or three hens. The 1947 Census Report[3] shows the Colony's total number of 'Malay' and 'Other Malaysian' rearers of poultry and livestock to be only 67.

Houses. The large majority of houses in Malay rural areas were little more than shacks. They consisted of planks of wood and a thatch roof, assembled in a day or two by the owner with the help of kinsmen and fellow-villagers. In Tanjong in 1950 in spite of the high cost of timber, three houses were built at an average cost of $65 per house, including the price of the meal served to the owner's helpers. In the countryside building land had little value and if, as was the case in coastal villages, a house was built on the foreshore, the Crown had the freehold and leased the site at a peppercorn rent.

In some urban and suburban areas of the Island, and less frequently in rural areas, there were Malay houses soundly built with seasoned and carved timber which cost upwards of $500 to build even before the war, and which boasted the traditional verandah, sitting-room, and bedrooms, raised on stilts or posts, and a kitchen with a cement floor on ground level. These houses were very few in number, and rarely inhabited by one household; the owner usually let rooms.

---

[1] cf. H. S. Morris, *Report on a Melanau Sago-Producing Community in Sarawak*, London 1953, pp. 76 f., on *reta pusaka*.

[2] cf. E. R. Leach, *Social Science Research in Sarawak*, London 1950, p. 70, on *pesoka*.   [3] p. 519.

In the rural areas, those Singapore Malays born and bred in the house owned by their parents prized their home far above its actual value in cash. It was their only solid point of anchorage and it provided them with a sense of security which could not be easily over-estimated. Their home, even if a shack, was often the only fixed asset of which they could boast. One might think at first that it was not so much the wood and thatch which gave this feeling of security, as the fact of living in one's native village. However, when in Tanjong I met villagers living in other people's homes because they had not rebuilt their own after the Occupation, I was struck by the anxiety about their housing which these men and women often expressed. They told visitors that they were just squatting (*tumpang*) while trying to save money in order to erect their own house. On the other hand, there was always an unmistakable note of pride when a Singapore Malay said, 'The house I live in is my own.'

Furniture. The poorest Malay homes were bare, save for mats and pillows. In the wealthiest homes there were beds, wardrobes, dressing-tables, tables, chests of drawers, chairs, armchairs, and a wireless set. There existed, of course, variations between the two extremes.

Gold Jewelry was usually worn by women, and consisted of chains, lockets, rings, ear-rings, bracelets, clasps, and sets of brooches. Men rarely wore jewelry of any kind, apart from an odd ring.

Tools of Trade were generally cooking utensils in the case of food hawkers; sewing-machines in the case of seamstresses; metal tools in the case of craftsmen and mechanics; and boats and fishing tackle among fishermen.

As a rule, the bulk of a man's property had been acquired by his sole efforts, and the bulk of a woman's property by her husband's. (As we saw earlier, in 1947 only 3·6 per cent of Singapore Malay women were gainfully occupied.) When they marry for the first time, the average Malay couple own their personal clothing only, although the bride may have one or two modest items of jewelry such as a ring or a pair of ear-rings rarely worth more than $20. After husband and wife have been married for a few years and settled in a home of their own, the house he may have built and whatever furnishings it contains belong to both of them equally. On the other hand, any items which a woman has acquired during marriage from the exercise of a trade or profession, without the help of her husband, are exclusively her own, and he can claim no share in them. Whatever property an individual has acquired before marriage (by gift, inheritance, or personal effort) remains exclusively his own. Any tools of trade which a man has acquired after his marriage from his sole earnings are his exclusive property. Any jewelry, however valuable, which a man has bought from his own earnings and given to his wife become her property. Children have no claims, *inter vivos*, on their parents' property.

2. Inheritance

There seemed to be no tradition for a man to accumulate capital with the express intention of leaving it as a trust for his children and grand-children or for his widow. I did not come across any implicit attitude or explicit statements to the effect that it is a person's duty to make such a provision.

If, as was usual, a Singapore Malay died intestate, the law was that his property be divided among his heirs according to Islam—a male heir being granted double the share of a female, where both are related to the deceased in the same degree. In practice, however, the heirs divided the estate according to *adat*. The bulk of Malay estates were too small in value to require formal administration, and litigation between the various heirs was rare. Generally, the sons inherited the tools and personal clothing of their father, while the daughters inherited the furniture, and the clothing and jewelry of their mother. If there was orchard land, all the children had equal rights to it.[1] If there was a house, it also belonged equally to all the children, but any unmarried children had preferential rights of occupation. If all the children were married and settled in independent accommodation, they usually reached some agreement as to which one among them would live in the house. If they could not agree, or if the house was in a dilapidated condition, or inconveniently situated for all of them, they might sell it and divide the amount equally between them. It was rare for an old couple to live alone, however, and usually the youngest daughter after her marriage remained with her parents. After the latter's death, it was customary for the woman and her household to continue living in the house, with the consent of her siblings, and without paying them rent. However, she paid for the replacements of timber and thatch, and for any other repairs.

After a man's death his widow retained in her lifetime ownership and control of the house (if he had built it during their union), and of house-hold goods. If her adult children gave her no economic assistance, she could sell items of furniture in order to buy essential food and clothing; she could also sell the house itself, although in practice she almost never did so. If a house had belonged to a man before his marriage, after his death his widow had rights of occupation which were superior to those of his adult children, but she could not dispose of the property. It was their inheritance. The same applied, *mutatis mutandis*, to a house which had belonged to a woman before her marriage: the widower held it in trust for her children.

After his wife's death a man retained ownership and control of the house he built before or during his marriage to her, and could dispose of it as he wished. However, he was unlikely to do so unless he urgently needed money to buy food and had no resources other than his house. The same

---

[1] cf. R. Winstedt, op. cit., p. 48. 'The Ninety-Nine Laws . . . lay down that when a person dies "house and garden, crockery, kitchen utensils and bedding are to be taken by the female children, iron tools or weapons, rice-fields and mines by the sons." ' See also E. N. Taylor, 'Malay Family Law', *Journal of the Royal Asiatic Society, Malayan Branch*, vol. xv, Part 1, May 1937.

was true of furniture and other household goods acquired during the marriage; whenever possible they were kept for his daughters.

If a widower remarried, his second wife and any children he had by her had no right of ownership in the house he had built during his earlier marriage, or in the furniture and household goods he had bought during the earlier union. They had only rights of use. The household of the Tanjong headmaster in 1950 showed these principles at work. The man had four children by his first wife, two sons and two daughters; and when she died during the war, he remarried. By his second wife he had a small son and an infant girl. His eldest daughter was married, and she lived in the house her father had built for her own mother. He in turn was living with his second wife and with his five children by the two unions in Government quarters. He was nearing retirement and due to vacate his present accommodation, and was therefore considering building another house for himself and his present wife and their children. A sewing-machine which he had bought for his first wife was used by his second wife; his older daughters did not know how to cut and make clothes, and their stepmother sewed for them. However, she would frequently comment that she wanted her husband to buy her a machine of her own, since her step-daughters might one day ask her to return their mother's machine to them. She would say, '*Dia punya*, it is their own.'

Any child taken in full adoption has in *adat* the same property and inheritance rights as a begotten child. In Islam, however, adopted children are barred entirely (unless, of course, they are also consanguineous kin, in which case they inherit according to their status as consanguineous kin). When a Malay died intestate in Singapore, therefore, and his estate was formally administered, adopted children were left without a share. Most Malays, however, did not take advantage of the law to flout long-established *adat* tenets.

3. *Economic Relationships in the Household*

Division of Labour. The household of Singapore Malays is not a unit of production. There are exceptions, of course, such as when a father and his sons fish together and pool their earnings, and the mother and her daughters help to make and mend nets. This, however, is rare. On the other hand, the household is a unit of consumption. The earnings are spent mainly on food which is eaten by all the members, irrespective of whether they are con-tributors to the household's income. The wage-earners are normally adult men, while women and girls are engaged in the 'non-gainful' occupations of housework and care of small children.

Husband-Wife Relationship. Where control over the household's income is concerned, there were two different types of arrangement according as to whether the husband's wages were paid daily or monthly. (Weekly wages were almost unknown in the Colony.) If his earnings were daily, as in the case of fishermen, hawkers, and some labourers, it was common for the husband to give his wife all his earnings when he came home. Whenever possible, the woman gave her husband some money to buy cigarettes, or a snack. Husbands who attempted to 'cheat' by keeping some money for themselves were, if found out, severely reprimanded by their wives for deceit and selfishness.

When men were monthly wage-earners, the position differed. Local shopkeepers (normally Indian or Chinese) usually gave them goods on credit. The common practice was for such households to take rice, the staple food, and all groceries on credit; the amount due (or a large proportion of it) was paid at the end of the month. When a man received his wages he first settled his account with the local shopkeeper himself, or else gave his wife the sum necessary for doing so. There was then a small range of variation as to what he did with the balance of the money. Sometimes he gave it all to his wife and she in turn allowed him a sum for his personal expenses, such as cigarettes, coffee, snacks and fares. This arrangement was not very common, however. More frequently, he kept the balance and gave her either about a dollar or so a day with which to buy fresh fish and vegetables—which the local shop did not normally stock—or else $5 or $6 every few days. (The exact amount of course varied according to the income and the size of the household.) Apart from that, should his wife need clothes for herself or their children, or any other extra item of expenditure, he provided her with the money required if he had it. It was rare for a Malay woman not to know the exact wage of her husband, and if she found that he spent on himself more than she thought he should, she did not hesitate to complain, for it was generally agreed that a man's first duty was not to himself, but to his wife and children. Bitter conjugal quarrels occurred if a man spent a large share of his capital or of his earnings without his wife's approval.

Sometimes a married woman earned money by working as a domestic servant, making food snacks, dressmaking, or trading. She had an exclusive right to the earnings, and apart from cases where her husband was temporarily ill or out of work, she used the money not on household expenditure but to buy herself and her children clothes and gold jewelry. If a man was out of work over a long period (such as a year or more), it was not common for his wife to seek employment and thus help to support him. Usually she obtained a divorce on the grounds of non-maintenance, and then looked for another suitable marriage partner. This was sometimes the case even if the man's unemployment was due not to laziness, but to ill-health. Many Singapore Malays asserted that a marriage relationship may mysteriously cause chronic ill-health in either spouse, and that as soon as there is a divorce the patient recovers; a woman who had become impatient of maintaining and nursing an invalid husband often gave this reason to explain her divorce.

One of the most common methods of saving was the buying of gold jewelry for women. Men did not spend a great deal of money on rings or chains or brooches for their small daughters, but they did for their wives, and this may seem difficult to understand since such jewelry remains a woman's personal and inalienable property. True, if the marriage endured and the man was in financial difficulties his wife did not hesitate to pawn, and later to sell, the gold ornaments, and to give him the money or to spend it on food and rent. However, if he divorced her or if she left him, she usually retained all the items.[1]

The outside observer may think it odd that in a society where marriages are highly unstable, men should invest their hard-earned capital in such an insecure fashion. There are reasons for it. The average husband values his wife's love too much to deny her the pleasure and pride of wearing valuable jewelry, and he may be unable to resist her persistent nagging; while some men fear that such a denial might precipitate a breakdown of the marriage, and they do not always consider divorce and separation from their children with equanimity. Moreover, a bejewelled wife is the best advertisement of a man's prosperity, and a great source of prestige for him. Men therefore continue to use much of their surplus income for the acquisition of gold trinkets for their wives, and they appear to shut off from their minds the likelihood that in the near or distant future they may be deprived simultaneously of wife and savings.

Such behaviour is not as rash as it might seem. A divorced woman is left in a precarious financial position, and if there are young children of the union the father is usually quick to abandon his legal and moral responsibility to maintain them. During the interim period between a woman's divorce and her remarriage, therefore, it is important that she have some assets which she can easily liquidate in order to support herself and her children in case her immediate kin are unable to be of great assistance, and her personal jewelry stands her in good stead. I heard several divorced men explain their neglect to maintain their children with the statement that they had well provided their ex-wives with jewelry, which should now be sold to feed their children.

Parents-Children. Parents fed, clothed, sheltered and nursed their children in infancy and childhood, gave them pocket-money, and paid for their religious education. Young children, on the other hand, performed services inside and outside the house to help their parents. When they reached puberty the girls remained at home and devoted their energies to domestic occupations. In some cases young girls earned money by taking in sewing at home, and with this money their mother usually bought them clothes. Adolescent boys went out to work, and gave part of their earnings to their mother towards their keep.

A young married couple often lived with the wife's parents, and the practice was for the man to pay his mother-in-law a fixed amount for his wife's board and his own. The balance of what he earned was spent as he and his wife wished, on clothes, jewelry, or outings.

[1] For an exception to this rule, see below, p. 125.

In households consisting of a divorcée or widow and young children, the woman went out to work and entrusted her older daughters with all the responsibilities of housekeeping. If the mother had a son who was a wage-earner, he sometimes gave her the bulk of his wages and she took part-time employment if it was necessary for her to supplement the amount.

Young men in the coastal areas, where the main economy was fishing, remained economically tied to their parents longer than those living in the Municipality or in the suburbs and employed as wage-earners. A young fisherman started going to sea with no capital equipment of his own, and with no skill. When he went in his father's or older brother's boat, he had no fixed share in the catch. When the fish was sold to a dealer, the money was given *in toto* to the boy's mother, and out of it she gave a small sum to her husband or older son for tobacco and pocket-money, and an even smaller sum to her younger boy. It takes at least three or four years for an adolescent boy to acquire sufficient skill at sea to enable him to go out alone, or with a younger boy, or on equal terms with another fisherman, and usually by that time he has reached his early twenties and there is talk of marriage for him. In such an event, of course, the sum required for the *bĕlanja kahwin* (marriage expenses) and for other costs incidental to the wedding must be found by the man's parents, as the prospective groom has not usually been able to accumulate any capital whatsoever. He knows that his parents may not have the whole amount required for the numerous ceremonies, but he also knows that their credit is better than his, and that they can obtain substantial sums from kinsmen and loans from friends. Until a fisherman marries, therefore, he remains largely under parental tutelage.

When a Singapore Malay marries, his first duty—as we saw—is to his wife and children. Therefore, when married sons wanted to give money to their parents, they often did so without their wife's knowledge, lest she complain. However, if a married child's parents are destitute, he or she must help to maintain them. This was stated as a strong principle of Malay custom, *adat*. It is, of course, also a tenet of Islam, as S. Vesey-Fitzgerald says:[1]

'Adult children are bound to maintain their parents, but not their step-parents, and according to Hanafi and Shafii law they are bound to maintain their grandparents. . . . These obligations are without distinction of sex or religion and are on the conditions only that the person to be maintained is unable to support himself without assistance, and that the person chargeable possesses more than is necessary for the maintenance of himself and his household. Even if he does not, he should admit to his house and table those who are indigent and cannot work. The duty to ancestors is considered stronger than the duty towards adult descendants.'

In cases of full adoption from early infancy (as of Chinese baby girls), the child was cared for as an own child and when it grew up had towards

[1] S. Vesey-Fitzgerald, op.cit., p. 98.

his adoptive parents the duties of an own child. However, if the adopted child was a Malay, full and unconditional adoption rarely occurred, and when it did the natural family of the child still kept in touch with it at regular, if even distant, intervals. Nevertheless, if a Malay had been adopted from early infancy and lived with his adoptive family continuously up to the age of marriage, it was unhesitatingly stated that his first duties were towards his adoptive parents since it was they who had fed him and brought him up.[1] If ever a person abused his authority over his employee, pupil or friend, the most common retort on the part of the victim or of onlookers was, 'What right has he to behave with such boldness? He has not given food, has he? (*Bukan dia ada kasi makan*).'

4. *Economic Relationships in the Larger Kin Group*

Joint Ownership. We know that among Singapore Malays there are no definable large kin groups except with reference to Ego or to a group of siblings, and that one Malay belongs to several Ego-centered groups of kin. This fact, however, does not preclude the existence of a large group of kinsmen owning property in common. There may be an 'inheritance group' of kinsmen (to whom, as we saw above, the term *waris* is applied). Several individuals may hold property which they have inherited from a common ancestor; they are not always very close kinsmen, and they may not have shared out the property among themselves for the simple reason that the inheritance is not easily divisible. In the Tanjong area, for instance, some fourteen descendants of a man who died at the close of the last century held a joint interest in a piece of land. The land had been leased by him to a Chinese shopkeeper who agreed to pay a fixed sum—$60—as annual rent. The shopkeeper built a wooden house on the plot to serve as shop, storeroom, and living accommodation. Later both owner and ground tenant died, and their property passed to their respective heirs. In 1950 the grandson of the shopkeeper continued to pay rent to the fourteen Malay descendants who owned the land jointly. He paid it to them as a group, every year, through the person designated by them. They included grandchildren and great-grandchildren of the Malay who originally granted the lease, and they lived some of them in Tanjong, some in islets off the coast. Admittedly, cases such as these are not numerous, but they exist.

A Malay may also hold property jointly with several different groups of kinsmen. Thus a widow may hold a share with her siblings and with the children of her dead siblings in a house left by her parents. She may also have inherited part of her husband's share in some acres of orchard land which he held jointly with his brothers and sisters and with the children of his dead siblings. This would be in addition to other property

---

[1] cf. the Corsican proverb quoted in a similar context by Radcliffe-Brown, *chiamu babba a chi me da pane. African Systems of Kinship and Marriage*, edited by A. R. Radcliffe-Brown and Daryll Forde, London 1950, p. 4.

which she may hold with other kinsmen engaged with her in a business venture.

Here it becomes necessary to distinguish joint property which is exploited in common from joint property which requires no effort for its maintenance. The instance of the Chinese shopkeeper's ground rent payments is an example of the latter, while an example of the former would be the ownership by a group of kinsmen of a net with which they fish, or of an eating-house in which they are the cooks and waiters. Because of the intense individualism of Singapore Malays and of their lack of tradition for corporate action generally, there are few enduring business partnerships among kinsmen, and even fewer among strangers. I heard of several cases of kinsmen who embarked hopefully together on a commercial undertaking, only to dissolve it a few months later. This occurred, for instance, in the case of three first cousins who started a hawker's stall; and of a woman and her mother's sister who bought sarongs and sold them on credit on regular door-to-door expeditions in various districts. There would be disagreement about the hours of work, or about the proportions of profit to be shared and to be re-invested in the enterprise, and soon they would decide that the best way out was to wind up the business and divide the assets. Informants assured me that partnerships among *orang lain* were even more precarious, as a Malay rarely has trust in the good faith of a non-kinsman.

In Tanjong it was obvious to any outsider as well as to the fishermen themselves that there were great opportunities open to them if they would pool their labour and resources. The men were engaged in two main types of fishing, line fishing (*panching*), and fishing with drift nets (*jaring hanyut*). Each *jaring hanyut* required at least two men to operate it. Whether they used nets or lines men usually went fishing in pairs. They were all of the opinion that the drift-net method was on the whole more profitable, but drift nets were expensive ($250-$300 each). Apart from the initial cost of the net there was the expense of maintaining it: periodical soaking in white of egg and oil, and repairs when it was torn. Several fishermen, therefore, used drift nets belonging to Chinese dealers on an adjacent island. The dealer received one third of the total catch in payment for the use of his net, and the other two thirds were shared equally by the two fishermen who had operated the net. However, they had to sell their own share to the same dealer, at his price, which was consistently lower than that which they would have got from other local dealers. If they tried to 'cheat' (or, as they put it, *jual black market*, sell black market), and were found out, the dealer would withdraw his net and other dealers would be reluctant to trust them. This had already happened to some Tanjong men who now went line fishing.

Frequently I would suggest that several fishermen—either friends or kinsmen—could easily save $250 in a few months, acquire a net, and either use it together in turn, or hire it out to fellow villagers. The fishermen would agree that this was feasible, but invariably added, 'Yes this is quite true, but we just do not come together, there is no co-operation, *ta' ada pakat*.' Certainly, a Fishermen's Co-operative Society for that area, started under Government auspices after the war, had evoked little enthusiasm.[1]

I asked whether any informal group of fishermen had ever tried to acquire a net jointly, and I was told that they had indeed tried but not succeeded. One man would change his mind after the others had started saving for a month, while another man would use his share of the savings to buy food for his household. There was not one instance they could record of joint acquisition of a drift net.

When examining the basis on which a fisherman selected his partner, I found that this was usually friendship or compatibility as much as kinship relations. Skill was not, it appeared, an important factor because there was no great variation in expertness among adult men. When they went line fishing they shared equally in the total catch, irrespective of whether one had caught more fish than the other. Two first cousins or brothers might go fishing together for about a week, and then each would go with a different partner, either a kinsman or a stranger. (Raymond Firth in his study of fishermen in Malaya also found that crews were not primarily organized on the basis of kinship relations.[2])

To summarize. There are few instances of property held jointly by a group of kinsmen. When joint property requires exploitation in common, it is of course essential that the owner-managers agree as to general policy. Singapore Malays claim that such harmony is rare among kinsmen and almost non-existent among strangers, and that men generally attach so much value to personal independence that they subordinate financial gain to it.

Mutual Assistance. There are strong moral notions involved in economic assistance to kinsmen. A man who has enough to eat and who can decently clothe himself and support the dependents in his household should help with gifts or loans a truly needy kinsman. It is good, *baik*, to do so; it is also *adat Mělayu*. However, it is not the duty of a Singapore Malay to do more than help his close *saudara* with essential food and clothing. A clerk, schoolteacher, or successful shopkeeper may, and does, enjoy living in a well-built house with sound furniture and with such luxuries as a wireless set, while his brother or sister or first cousin, and their children, live precariously on the wages received as domestic servants or labourers, and no one in the community expects the more prosperous person to share his well-earned possessions with his less fortunate kinsmen. It was only in a real crisis, such as ill health or indebtedness due to unemployment or a confinement, that the richer was in duty bound to help the poorer.

[1] Raymond Firth found that co-operative Malay associations for fish marketing were not very successful in Malaya. (*Malay Fishermen: Their Peasant Economy*, London 1946, p. 62.)   [2] op. cit., pp. 105-6.

There were three spheres where mutual assistance among kinsmen was most manifest: monetary loans and gifts; services; and manner of apportioning a common inheritance. Outside the circle of the simple family, a man who had any means usually helped kinsmen who were hungry or infirm with food or money. This was particularly the case where his closest *saudara* were concerned: married children, parents, siblings, grandparents, grandchildren, parent's sibling, sibling's child, and first cousin, generally in that order. Whenever practicable he invited a destitute close relative to live in his home at least temporarily. More distant kinsmen had a lesser claim on one's generosity. Within the very close degrees, such as the first five just enumerated, no balance-sheet of gifts, loans, and debts was kept. No exact repayment in cash or kind or services was necessary. Sometimes the wealthier brother remained wealthy until his death, and the poorer brother poor. Sometimes also, the wealthier sister had to help her poorer sister with money as well as with services if the latter was ill or had several young children whom she could not care for without help.

Where affines were concerned, the spouses of one's children and of one's siblings were helped unhesitatingly when doing so resulted in direct benefit to one's own children and siblings. The parents and siblings of a man's wife were also entitled to his economic assistance if they were in acute need. A married woman had a great measure of authority concerning the manner in which her husband's income was spent, and she could insist on coming to the aid of her own parents or siblings. Most Malay husbands in Singapore did not refuse such help; they remembered that in the first years of their marriage they had been treated with generosity by their parents-in-law. More distant affines were entitled to preferential treatment over strangers.

In this whole complex of mutual assistance the gap between theory and practice was small. There were few complaints about the selfishness or lack of generosity of one's close kinsmen. On the other hand, there were frequent references to help received in illness, unemployment, or widowhood. A regular comment was, '*Adat orang Mĕlayu, saudara tolong mĕnolong*, it is the custom of Malays for kinsmen to help one another.'

We saw earlier that generally Singapore Malay estates were divided not according to Islam, but according to *adat*. Division according to *adat*, however, took place as a rule if none of the heirs was very poor or destitute. When the moment of sharing their deceased parents' property arrived, wealthier siblings usually surrendered part or all of their share in *adat* in favour of a poorer sibling because they took pity on him or her, *kasihan sama dia*. Not all Singapore Malays behaved in this manner, however, and therefore one cannot say that there were three clear-cut principles, Muslim law enforceable by the courts of the Colony, *adat* law, and local practice. Muslim law and *adat* law were duly recognized and differentiated by the people themselves, but 'local' practice varied not according to the various districts of the Colony, or according to whether the people concerned were

Mĕlayu bĕtul or Indonesian immigrants, but according to the degree of kindliness or generosity of the individuals concerned.

5. *Nepotism*

Opportunities to place kinsmen existed mainly in the field of casual or unskilled labour, and in occupations which required little training, such as that of office messenger. Where skilled work was concerned, it was in the selection of apprentices that nepotism could thrive. Employers had little direct contact with the labour market, it was impractical for them to advertise (the majority of workers were only half literate and did not read newspapers), and so they relied on their foremen to find suitable young recruits.

Among Singapore Malays (and many Singaporeans said this was also true of other ethnic groups in the Colony), nepotism was a recognized practice. Those who deplored it tended to be unsuccessful candidates. Further, when a workman was dismissed he usually assumed that the foreman's motive was to create a vacancy for a kinsman.[1]

When I lived on an urban estate housing a large proportion of Malay labourers, I was constantly made aware of the importance of kinship relations among workmen themselves and between workmen and supervisory staff. Wives and children took an active part in the arguments to which a reprimand or a dismissal led, and it was rare indeed for such arguments not to centre around the theme of nepotism. The foreman's wife would be involved in acrimonious disputes with the female kin of a man whom her husband had reported for inefficiency or absenteeism. The foreman's children would be slighted in the street or in the local shop by the children of a man whom he had caused to be dismissed, and the foreman's family generally feared any possible effects of spells which the injured man might cause to be cast in revenge. Even if the person who replaced the dismissed workman was not known to be related in any way to the foreman or to his wife, it was common to insist that he must be a *saudara*.

On one such occasion I challenged the wife of the dismissed man to establish any kinship link, especially as I knew a great deal about the circumstances of the dismissal. (The man had absented himself repeatedly without valid cause and had been impertinent to an inspector, who had instructed the Malay foreman to terminate the employment.) She replied that she did not know the precise way in which the foreman and the new labourer were connected, but that she had it on very good authority that the two men had been extremely friendly for many years and exchanged visits, and that such friendship and familiarity must spring from the fact

---

[1] An extension of the same principle operated in cases where a Chinese or Indian foreman dismissed a Malay workman. The latter assumed that the foreman was trying to replace Malays by persons of his own 'race'. Such an assumption was not always unjustified.

that they were *saudara*. She added that there were several labourers on the estate who were kinsmen of the foreman himself or connected affinally to his wife or to the spouses of his children, and she proceeded at once to mention them, one by one. Paradoxically enough, the foreman and his wife were in turn attacked by some of their *saudara* who were seeking employment from the same concern, on the grounds that he did not intercede on their behalf. One of the great advantages of the work was the provision of excellent housing on the estate at a nominal rent, and this more than compensated for the low wages (about $50 a month) paid to the labourers.

Where the Civil Service was concerned, there were very few opportunities open to Malays in Singapore to exercise nepotism; senior posts in the Administration were held by Britons, Chinese and Eurasians. Only a handful of Malays were employed in other than junior clerical positions; the majority were messengers, drivers, and the like. The few who had risen to a senior grade complained that they were constantly besieged by kinsmen with requests for assistance to secure Government employment. The one Department about which I heard persistent allegations of nepotism was the Education Department, which in 1950 employed about 260 Malay schoolteachers in the Colony's vernacular schools. Some schoolteachers claimed that favouritism was shown in posting and promotion, but I was unable to ascertain whether such accusations were based on fact.

Another sphere of employment where allegations of nepotism were frequent was domestic service. I heard, for instance, that a nursemaid found constant fault with a washerwoman if the latter had not been chosen by her, and would cause her to be dismissed; then she would introduce a kinswoman as a replacement. Cooks, gardeners, houseboys and drivers were accused of similar intrigues.

In the whole sphere of nepotism there were two conflicting moral principles which were separately but explicitly stated by Singapore Malays. One was that solidarity among *saudara* should take precedence over other considerations; and the other that such solidarity must not prejudice the rights of others, of *orang lain*, in such crucial situations as earning one's living. A person expected to be shown favour by a kinsman in securing employment,[1] but he strongly resented being refused a job because another applicant with equal or inferior merits had been thus favoured. Few candidates seemed aware of the contradiction inherent in this attitude.

The tendency to exaggerate the incidence of nepotism and the extent of competition for urban jobs had sad effects. Some young boys in the rural areas who were exceptionally ambitious and eager to learn a trade were discouraged by the older villagers' wise statements that nobody can find an opening as an apprentice in factory or workshop if there is no kinsman

[1] cf. Olga Lang, *Chinese Family and Society*, New Haven 1946, pp. 181-92, where the author discusses similar attitudes among the Chinese.

or corrupt acquaintance willing to help. Most of the adolescents accepted the position with some bitterness and unhappily followed the precarious occupation of their fathers: fishing, rubber-tapping, or gathering and chopping firewood. Boys in the town, however, had more opportunities because they were more sophisticated and because they were more likely to have friends and neighbours as well as kinsmen in the trade they wished to enter who were willing to give them reliable information and help in applying for employment.

3

The Household

THROUGHOUT Singapore the residential and economic unit of the Malays is, of course, the household. Further, since the structure of the kinship system is bilateral, the only crystallized kinship unit readily observable is in the household.

The poorest homes were bare; in them there was no furniture, only bedding which consisted of old and worn pandanus mats and kapok pillows, and a few cooking utensils and plates; clothes were kept in a neat pile on a shelf or in a small basket. There were three such homes in Tanjong and I also saw many more in the Municipality. The inhabitants were acutely aware of the shabbiness in which they lived and spontaneously commented upon it and apologized when a newcomer came to visit them.

In both the rural and urban areas, one item of furniture was considered extremely important: a large bed, usually a four-poster, neatly covered with sheets and frills. This bed was rarely used to sleep on; it existed essentially for show purposes and had pride of place in the house. Most Malays slept on mats or on kapok mattresses on the floor. In the morning the bedding was neatly rolled and stacked against a wall. Other items found in many Malay homes were small dressing tables and crude wooden tables and chairs. Only the more prosperous inhabitants had in addition armchairs, wardrobes, and wireless sets.

In the villages and in some parts of the town where there was no electricity the type of lamp used for lighting was a means of assessing the economic position of the household. A pressure kerosene lamp of foreign manufacture, costing about $30, was owned by a limited number. The majority used small kerosene wick lamps which cost less than one dollar and consumed less fuel than the other variety, while of course giving a much poorer light.

The interior of the average Malay home was neat and tidy, the floor being swept several times a day, and every member of the household showed interest in the general appearance of the rooms. Housework and cooking were essentially female occupations, but a man could often be seen removing crumbs from the floor after a meal, or tidying the house.

Children up to the age of five or six years slept with their parents on the same mat or mattress, or in close proximity to them on different mats. If they were older, they slept further away in the same room. From about the age of twelve years, children slept in a different room from their parents if there was one available; otherwise a partition, usually consisting of an old sheet hanging on a line across the room, was made at night to separate parents and grown children. If there were adolescent or adult children of both sexes in the household, it was usual for the father and sons to sleep at one end of the room, and the mother and daughters at another end.

Food was generally eaten in the kitchen, unless there were guests or unless the kitchen was very small or inconvenient. There were serving spoons for rice and the other dishes, but Malays used the fingers of their right hand to eat with. Small children were fed separately, either before or after the grown-ups, so that they might not disturb them at meals. It was traditional for a newly-wed couple to eat together only for the first few weeks if they lived in the same household as their parents; if they lived alone they continued to eat together until the first child was born. Often, then, the wife ate separately. If it was a large household the custom was that the mother and daughters ate together, as did the father and grown sons, with the latter usually taking precedence in time (and sometimes in choice morsels) over the female members. However, there were many variations according to the type and hours of work of the men, and to individual preferences.

On ceremonial occasions such as weddings, the men guests were served before the women guests. If crockery and domestic help were plentiful, the men and the women might be served simultaneously, but this was extremely rare. It was unheard of for female guests to be served before male guests.

I here define a household as a group of people who live in the same house and engage in a large number of common activities as well as sharing a common budget. This definition of household applies also to cases where a few items of housekeeping—such as rice—are bought separately by some members, as long as a large number of other items (such as fish, vegetables, fats, sugar, coffee, fuel, etc.) are bought from a common budget.[1]

The household unit of Singapore Malays most frequently consists of a married couple living together with their unmarried children. This is the unit which is usually referred to as the simple, elementary, or nuclear, family. The head of the household is the chief wage-earner, and in the overwhelming majority of cases, a man. This is so since only a negligible percentage of the female population is gainfully employed.[2]

When there are other people living with a simple family in a household, usually they are closely related either to the husband or to the wife, or to both. For instance, common additions are a married daughter with her husband and perhaps their small baby; a sibling or a parent of either the husband or the wife; an orphaned or destitute child of a sibling of the husband or the wife. It is rare to find more distant kinsmen than those

---

[1] For a more detailed discussion of this point, see below p. 62.
[2] See above p. 6.

enumerated above (such as cousins, great-aunts or great-uncles of the married couple) living permanently with the family, while total strangers, such as lodgers, are extremely rare. There are also other types of household grouping, for instance single male 'households', especially in the case of immigrant Indonesians of recent settlement in the Colony; households consisting of a group of orphaned unmarried siblings; and households where the chief wage-earner is a woman who is widowed or divorced and lives with her young children whom she supports. These last two types of household may be called a *denuded simple family*[1] because they consist of the simple family from whom one or both parents are absent. The term, however, would not apply to a simple family household where one or more children are absent on account of emigration, marriage, death or adoption. So long as the parents continue to live together with at least one unmarried child, the household is of the simple family type. The presence of offspring of the married couple in the household is essential: a married couple without a child do not constitute a family. Strictly speaking, of course, if a married couple's children are dead, or have left the parental home in order to settle in other households, the parents living alone could be justifiably described as a *denuded simple family*. I have not done so in the following statements and tables of household composition, however, but have labelled households where husband and wife live alone as 'Married Couples', irrelevantly of whether the wives have or have not borne children of the union. This has been necessary because in the survey of the Municipality of Singapore there is no information on that score.

My analysis of the household composition of Singapore Malays is based on two sources. The first is my own survey of Tanjong; the statement on household composition gives details of all the forty-eight Malay households of that fishing village in August 1949. I had been living there since March of that year and was able to gather personally all the relevant information.

The second statement is derived from the schedules prepared by the Singapore Social Welfare Department for the compilation of its *Social Survey of Singapore, 1947*. The Department used a random sample of 4,965 households in the Municipal area: these included Chinese, Malay, European, Eurasian and Other households. The definition of a household was that of 'a group of persons who eat together or share in common house-keeping expenditure.'[2] It was also stated that 'It is possible for a single-person to constitute a household.'[3] The fact that I have defined a household as a group of people who live in the same house as well as maintaining a joint housekeeping budget, and that I have used this definition in my analysis of household composition in Tanjong, does not invalidate a com-

---

[1] cf. Rosemary Firth's *denuded individual family*. Rosemary Firth, *Housekeeping Among Malay Peasants* (London School of Economics Monographs on Social Anthropology No. 7), London 1943, p. 7.
[2] *Social Survey*, p. 27.   [3] *Social Survey*, p. 138.

parison between the statements of household composition. In Tanjong, in every case, the group of people who ate together or shared in common housekeeping expenditure were also the group who lived together in the same house.

The Singapore Social Welfare Department kindly gave me access to the original schedules and I analysed those relating to Malaysian (i.e. both local and immigrant) households.[1]

It was unfortunately not possible for the Survey to cover in great detail the kinship relations which every member of the household bore to the head. Thus under 'Children' one supposedly finds children of the couple, adopted children, and children of either party by a former marriage. 'Simple families' in the context of this Municipal or urban survey, then, must refer to those households which consist of a man, his wife, and the children of either or both, whether own or adopted children.

TABLE I. Types of Household

		Percentages		Number of Households	
		Municipality	Tanjong	Municipality	Tanjong
1.	Simple Family	37·4	54·2	214	26
2.	Married Couples	8·7	4·2	50	2
3.	Denuded S.F.	8·2	16·7	47	8
4.	Denuded S.F. + kin	3·3	12·6	19	6
5.	S.F. + kin	12·1	6·3	69	3
6.	Single-Male	24·3	2	139	1
7.	Single-Female	1·9	2	11	1
8.	Polygynous	0·4	0	2	0
9.	Unspecified	3·7	0	21	0
10.	S.F. + lodger	0	2	0	1
	Total	100%	100%	572	48

TABLE II. Individuals Living in Different types of Household

		Percentages		Number of Individuals in Households	
		Municipality	Tanjong	Municipality	Tanjong
1.	Simple Family	47·2	60·5	952	124
2.	Married Couples	5	1·9	100	4
3.	Denuded S.F.	6·8	13·2	137	27
4.	Denuded S.F. + kin	4·6	12·7	93	26
5.	S.F. + kin	22·3	6·3	450	13
6.	Single-Male	6·9	0·5	139	1
7.	Single-Female	0·5	0·5	11	1
8.	Polygynous	0·9	0	18	0
9.	Unspecified	5·8	0	117	0
10.	S.F. + lodger	0	4·4	0	9
	Total	100%	100%	2,017	205

[1] The published Social Survey figure for Malaysian households is 580. However, I was able to trace only 572 relevant schedules.

HOUSEHOLD COMPOSITION IN TANJONG

14 *Simple Families.* **71** *individuals.*

14 households consist of a husband, wife, and the couple's own children (4 households of 4 individuals each; 6 households of 5; 3 households of 6; and one household of 7).

12 *Simple Families* (*Wider Sense of Term*). **53** *individuals.*

3 households consist of a husband, wife, and their adopted children (2 households of three persons, and one household of four persons). Total: 10 individuals.

4 households consist of a husband, wife, their own children, and their adopted children (3 households of four individuals and one household of five). Total: 17 individuals.

1 household: husband, wife and children of husband's first marriage (four individuals).

1 household: husband, wife, children of the couple, and children of the wife's former marriage (5 individuals).

1 household: husband, wife, children of the couple, and children of the husband's former marriage (7 individuals).

1 household: husband, wife, and their adopted child; wife's child by a first marriage; husband's adopted daughter of earlier marriage (5 individuals).

1 household: husband, wife, own young child and adopted child; husband's daughter by a former marriage (5 individuals).

2 *Married Couples only.* **4** *individuals.*

2 households consisting each of a married couple living alone.

8 *Denuded Simple Families.* **27** *individuals.*

4 households consist of a divorced or widowed woman and her own young dependent children (one household of 2 individuals, one of 3, one of 4, and one of 5). Total: 14 individuals.

1 household: a single man and his mother (2 individuals).

1 household: a single man, his mother, his two brothers, and his two adopted sisters (6 individuals).

1 household: a woman and her two young adopted children (3 individuals).

1 household: a man and his adult unmarried daughter (2 individuals).

6 *Denuded Simple Families and Other Kin.* **26** *individuals.*

1 household: a divorced man, his divorced sister and her child (3 individuals).

1 household: a widower, his brother's widow and this brother's son (3 individuals).

1 household: a single man, one widowed sister, one divorced sister and her adopted child (4 individuals).

1 household: a widower, his widowed sister and her two children (4 individuals).

1 household: a widow, her two young children, and her father (4 individuals).

1 household: a widower and his four unmarried children; his widowed daughter and her two children (8 individuals).

3 *Simple Families and Wife's Kin. 13 individuals.*

1 household: husband, wife, their adopted daughter, and wife's mother (4 individuals).

1 household: husband, wife, wife's adopted daughter, and wife's unmarried brother (4 individuals).

1 household: husband, wife, husband's adopted child of earlier marriage; and wife's mother and sister (5 individuals).

1 *Single-male Household. 1 individual.*

1 *Single-Female Household. 1 individual.*

1 *Simple Family and lodger. 9 individuals.*

1 household: husband, wife, and children of the couple; husband's children by a first marriage, wife's child by her first marriage; one male lodger (9 individuals).

Total Number of Households: 48. Total Number of Individuals: 205. Average Size of Household: 4·3 individuals.[1]

It will be seen that only fourteen households in Tanjong are of the simple family type as originally defined, of a married couple and the children of their union. However, in order to facilitate comparison with the urban survey schedules, I have added the other twelve cases where there are adopted children or stepchildren. Thus the total of Tanjong simple-family households becomes twenty-six.

There are two cases of married couples living alone: both had been recently married.

Then follow eight households of denuded simple families.

The fourth category is of six households, each consisting of one denuded simple family with siblings, parents, sibling's children, or a widowed child and grandchildren of the head of the household.

The fifth category consists in every case of a simple family with whom live relatives of the wife. In Tanjong there was no comparable category of a simple family with whom lived relatives of the husband.

Then come single-person 'households'. The man living alone had a married son in the village, but he had quarrelled with his son's wife three years earlier and lived separately. The woman living alone was middle-aged, her closest relatives in the village being the children of her dead first cousin. She had lost her mother and her children during the Japanese Occupation, had separated from her husband, and in 1947 lost her adopted daughter. She was now considering adopting another child.

Finally there is one household consisting of a simple family with a lodger who is not related by kinship to any member. This lodger was a pupil-teacher at the village school, and as his parents lived several miles away, he boarded with the family of the headmaster of the school. On school holidays he usually went to stay with his parents. In the month of August, during which this survey was taken, the school was functioning as usual.

[1] Figures here, as elsewhere, are given to the nearest first place of decimals.

E

HOUSEHOLD COMPOSITION IN THE MUNICIPALITY

214 *Simple Families*. 952 *individuals*.

214 households of simple families: a married couple with the unmarried children (own or adopted) of either or of both.

50 *Married Couples only*. 100 *individuals*.

50 households of married couples alone.

47 *Denuded Simple Families*. 137 *individuals*.

12 households: a married woman with her unmarried children. The husband in each case was an absentee wage-earner (32 individuals).

12 households: a widow or divorcée and her unmarried children (41 individuals).

9 households: a widowed or divorced man and his unmarried children (24 individuals).

14 households: an unmarried man and his mother and/or unmarried siblings (40 individuals).

19 *Denuded Simple Family and Other Kin*. 93 individuals.

19 households: a widowed, divorced, or separated man or woman with his/her unmarried children and various other kinsmen.

63 *Simple Families or Married Couples plus Kin of Husband and/or Wife*. 450 *individuals*.

(a) 13 households: a simple family or married couple and the wife's kinsmen.

(b) 33 households: a simple family or married couple and the husband's kinsmen.

(c) 5 households: a simple family and kinsmen of both the husband and the wife.

(d) 18 households: each constitute a group of related simple families, or of simple families and married couples.

139 *Single-Male Households*. 139 *individuals*.

11 *Single-Female Households*. 11 *individuals*.

2 *Polygynous Households*. 18 *individuals*.

2 households: each consists of a man, his two wives, and his children.

21 *Unspecified Households*. 117 *individuals*.

21 households where insufficient information is available.

Total Number of Households: 572. Total Number of Individuals: 2,017. Average Size of Household: 3·5 individuals.

The first two categories, of 214 simple-family households, and of 50 households consisting each of a married couple alone, require no immediate comment or elucidation.

In the third category of 47 households, I have thought it advisable to class together the four different types of denuded simple family, since in all the cases the household is composed of members who had been almost certainly living in a simple family until the parents separated, divorced, or died, or until a group of unmarried siblings lost both parents. In the group of 12 households consisting of a married woman and her children (husband an absentee wage-earner), the husband was a sailor in 7 cases. In the group of 12 households consisting of a woman living alone with her children, she was gainfully employed in 9 cases, and in 11 of the 12 cases all her children were under the age of sixteen.

The fourth category is constituted by 19 households which consist each of a denuded simple family, and siblings or a parent of the chief wage-earner; in some cases there are two closely related denuded simple families in the same household. As an instance of the first type is the household consisting of a widower and his small children with whom lives his own mother; as an instance of the second type is the household where a divorced man and his young children live with the man's widowed sister and her children.

The fifth category is subdivided into four groups, and it is interesting to analyse the composition of each group. In (a) there are 13 households of simple families or married couples with kinsmen of the wife. In five of these households there is the wife's sibling; in four, there is the wife's mother living with the simple family of her daughter; in two, there is the wife's mother and a sibling of the wife; and in the last two, there is the wife's father. Thus in none of the 13 households is there a more distant relative of the wife than a parent or a sibling. When we come to group (b), on the other hand, of 33 households where only the husband's kinsmen are resident members, we find that unmarried 'cousins' figure in five of the 33 households. The term cousin is not defined, so it must be presumed to refer to any type of cousin, parallel or cross-cousin, as well as first, second, or third cousin. In 16 households the husband's siblings only are the resident relatives; in 9, the husband's mother; in 2 households, the husband's mother and his younger siblings; and in the last household the husband's father lives with the simple family of his son. Group (c) is the smallest, with five households of simple families with kinsmen of both the husband and the wife. In two households live the husband's mother and his wife's siblings; in one household, the husband's 'aunt' and her young children, and his wife's mother; in one household, the husband's young nephew and nieces and the wife's grandmother; and in the last household are the husband's nephew and nieces, his cousin, and his wife's sister. In the last group, (d), of this category are 18 households. In seven cases, a married daughter lives with her husband and small children in the same household as that of her parents; but there are only two cases of a son and his own simple family living with the simple family of his parents. There is also one instance of a household where there live: (i) husband and wife with their unmarried children; (ii) their married daughter with her husband and young children; (iii) their married son with his wife only. Finally, there are six cases consisting each of a brother and a sister with their respective spouses and children in one household. The last two cases are of two male cousins living with their simple families in the same household.

The sixth and seventh categories are of single-person 'households'. Whereas only eleven women budget for food alone, one hundred and thirty-nine men do so. Only eighteen of the one hundred and thirty-nine men stated they were local Malays: the other 121 returned themselves as being Javanese, Boyanese, Sumatran, or just 'Indonesian'. Eight of the eleven women stated they were Javanese, Boyanese, or Indonesian, while the other three said they were local Malays.

In the eighth category are the only two polygynous households of the sample. However, this does not necessarily mean that only two of the total married males in the sample were engaged in polygynous unions; all it means is that only in two cases was there co-residence of a man and his wives. Of course, many of the immigrant Malays from Indonesia, married in Singapore and living in monogamous households in the Colony, may have been previously married in the country of their birth and may not have divorced their former wives, thus being polygynous in form. Apart from this, there is also the possibility of men in the sample maintaining two (or more) separate establishments for their two (or more) wives, in the Colony itself. Also some households of denuded simple families of a woman and her children, or females returned as not living with a husband, may in fact have been households supported by a polygynous man who lived elsewhere permanently with another wife.[1]

Finally there are twenty-one schedules with insufficient information available to classify them in any category: schedules which entirely omitted the relationship of one or more members to the head of the household, or insufficiently described them as 'relative' without specifying the degree of the kinship relation or stating whether the relative was the husband's or the wife's.

Before proceeding with a comparative analysis of the household composition in the two samples, I should like to make the following points clear. Not only is this a comparison between a rural and an urban sample, but also between a local Malay community on the one hand, and a mixed local-Malay and immigrant-Malay 'group' on the other hand. (In the Social Welfare Department Survey, households were classified as 'immigrant' or 'indigenous' according to the place of birth of the head of the household. The chief wage-earner was considered the head of the household.) Furthermore, the rural 'sample' is one of the total Malay population of one particular village, whereas the urban figures are those of a random sample from the urban area (the Municipality) of Singapore. Of 72,901 Malays living in the Municipality, 2,017 were represented in the sample, or less than 3 per cent. This means that when we deal with the rural figures we have accurate figures and percentages while in the case of the urban figures there is the possibility of slight errors which inevitably

_____
[1] I deal with the subject of polygyny in more detail in chapter 4 below.

occur in the process of sampling. Moreover, the two samples considerably differ in size: 48 versus 572 households; 205 versus 2,017 individuals.

Another obstacle to a comparison between the two sets of results is that in the Municipal Survey 'lodgers who were not relatives of the rest of the household were regarded as separate households whether they shared in a common table or not.'[1] This obstacle, however, is not as serious as might at first appear. In the first place, it will be remembered that in Tanjong there was only one individual who lived as a lodger. In the second place, an examination of the addresses of the different households in the schedule leads one to suppose that even in the Municipality the number of lodgers who are not related to the household members is small. Apart from single-person 'households', comparatively few households lived at the same address, and an overwhelming proportion of the one hundred and fifty individuals constituting single-person 'households' lived in lodging-houses. Also my own knowledge of household composition among Singapore Malays leads me to believe that it is extremely rare to find people who are not related by recognizable ties of kinship sharing housekeeping expenditure.

As far as patterns of differentiation in household composition between indigenous and immigrant groups are concerned, there are no significant variations, with one exception. This exception concerns single-person 'households', and as stated previously only 21 of the 150 individuals were indigenous. The remaining 129 (121 men and 8 women) returned themselves as Indonesians. There were lodging-houses in Singapore for Boyanese, Javanese, and other Malaysian immigrants who had recently arrived from their homeland to seek employment in the Colony. These men either sent for their wives after they found a job, or else married a Singapore Malay woman, and in both cases they tended to leave the lodging-house and seek accommodation elsewhere.

The fact that it is largely men and not women who live in single-person 'households' can be easily accounted for. Firstly, few women come to Singapore alone unless it is with the specific purpose of living with relatives, or joining their husbands or children. Secondly, it is considered unfortunate (and sometimes improper) for a woman to live alone if she has relatives living in the Island, in the Federation, or in some other part of the Malay world. For instance when a woman comes from, say, Java, where all her relatives live, in order to join her husband in Singapore and he later divorces her, she will either attempt to remarry quickly and stay on, or failing that, she usually sells her few personal belongings in order to pay for her fare back to her homeland.

The first obvious conclusion to draw from Tables I and II is that the most frequent type of household composition is that of the simple family consisting, in the extended sense, of a married couple and the unmarried, begotten or adopted children of either or of both persons. This type

[1] See *Social Survey of Singapore, 1947*, p. 7.

accounted for 26 out of 48 households in Tanjong, and for 214 out of 572 households in the Municipality. When we look at the number of individuals living in simple-family households, the significance of this pattern becomes still more apparent.

124 out of 205 individuals (60·5 per cent of the total population) lived in simple-family households in Tanjong.

952 out of 2,017 individuals (47·2 per cent of the total population) lived in simple-family households in the urban areas.

The fact that the figure for married couples living alone is considerably higher, proportionately, in the Municipality than it is in Tanjong may be due to several factors. Firstly, because of the urban survey definition of a household as a group of people who share in a common table, it may be that in cases where married couples live in the same house as their parents, but have, for some food items only, separate housekeeping arrangements, the couples have been entered as forming separate households. One difficulty in defining the phrase 'sharing in common housekeeping expenditure' is that it is very frequent among Singapore Malays for a married couple (or other persons) living with relatives to buy their rice separately and pay for it separately, although it is often cooked in the same pot as that of the rest of the household. The fact that rice, the staple, had been rationed during the last few years probably helped to intensify this practice, already frequent before the war. In such cases, it is possible that investigators were informed that the married couple had a separate housekeeping budget from the rest of the household. The common procedure, however, was for the couple to share in the cost of vegetables, spices, fish, cooking fuel and light with their other relatives while buying their rice separately.[1]

Rosemary Firth found a similar practice to prevail in Kelantan in 1939/40. She says:

'In some cases of separate budgeting in joint households, there would be a pooling of certain resources, especially fish, firewood, lamp oil, and sometimes betel and smoking requisites, but the staple, rice, would always be bought separately.'[2]

A second factor is that of housing. Malay tradition is that a newly-wed couple reside for the first few weeks or months in the home of the bride's parents, and often until after the first child of the union is born. On the other hand, the married couple should have a separate bedroom, or at least a separate cubicle. Under conditions of urban overcrowding, where

---

[1] Here it may be argued that the practice of buying rice separately but sharing in other domestic expenditure may also have led to other than married couples being listed as separate household units. This must be conceded.

[2] Rosemary Firth, op. cit., p. 9. The author also gives brief notes on different types of budgeting in joint households, pp. 9-12.

the bride's family may all be living in one room, it is clearly not practicable for the bridal pair to reside for more than a few days in the home of the bride, and so alternative accommodation has to be found. The problem rarely presents itself in a village, where the majority of people own a house which consists usually of more than one room. Moreover, if the house is too small, there is often sufficient land available to make an extension of another small room for the couple.

The third—and probably most important—factor making for the differential rate of separate residence of married couples arises from the varied occupational structure in the town. The man may have a job which requires him to reside in a specific area, or which supplies him with living quarters, some distance away from the home of his wife's parents or of his own parents. This is so in the case of policemen, of domestic servants, or drivers, and of some labourers. In point of fact, the occupation of several of the fifty men in the 'Married Couples Only' category was domestic service and driving motor vehicles.

Finally, there is the possibility that in some of these cases the couple have been married over a period of years and had lived with their own children in their household, but that at the time of the Survey the children were dead, or married, or living away from home.

In both Tables, denuded simple families are seen to be twice as common in Tanjong as they are in the Municipality. I think the main explanation for this again lies in the peculiarities of housing and close proximity of kinsmen in villages. In rural areas most simple families live in the houses they own, and when the father dies they do not have to move out, but they often do in town because they can no longer afford to pay the rent. Moreover, the members of a denuded simple family in a village usually have close relatives living nearby, perhaps as next-door neighbours, to whom they can appeal for help when needed. When a woman is left destitute with small children to support, in Tanjong she can leave the children with relatives in the daytime while she goes out to gather firewood for sale. In the Municipality, her relatives may live several miles away from her present home, so that she often goes to live permanently with a sister or another kinswoman who may look after her children while she herself goes out to work during the day.

When we come to consider households of simple families plus kinsmen, we find that whereas in the Municipality these relatives may be the husband's or the wife's, in Tanjong they are exclusively the wife's. This is probably because there are very few women who have come from outside in order to marry a Tanjong villager and live in his village. The pattern is the other way, a man from another village or nearby island coming to live in his wife's village with her parents at first, and later building a house there for them both. Consequently it is more common for a woman than it is for a man to have own relatives resident in the village. Moreover, if a man's parents or siblings become destitute they choose to continue living in their own village, partly supported there by a daughter or sister perhaps, rather than come to Tanjong, a foreign village, as poor relations. This situation would not arise, of course, in cases where both the husband and the wife are natives of Tanjong.

It is interesting to note that in a 'simple-family plus kin' household, whenever the kinsmen are the wife's, both in Tanjong and in the Municipality, they are her sibling or her parent (with only one exception in the Municipality of a wife's grandmother). On the other hand, whereas kinsmen of the husband are also most frequently a sibling or parent, they sometimes include more distant kinsmen such as 'cousins', 'nephews' and 'nieces', and 'aunts'. This is probably because only close relatives of a wife can claim to be partly or fully supported by her husband.

Fathers alone of either the husband or wife rarely live with the simple family of their child. This may be due partly to the fact that after middle age male mortality is higher than female mortality, and partly to the fact that after their early thirties Malay women have less opportunity to re-marry than men. It is probable, for instance, that in several cases of a mother living with the simple family of her child, the woman was divorced, while her ex-husband had remarried and was living in another household with his new wife. This hypothesis finds strong confirmation in a table in the Census Report for 1947.[1] For the total Malaysian (i.e., both indigenous and immigrant) population of the Federation and the Colony of Singapore, these are the percentages of married persons in the total of each sex in the three age-groups:

Age-group	Males	Females
15-34 years	48·4%	75·5%
35-44 years	89·4%	77·8%
45 and over	85·5%	43·3%

The balance in each age-group comprises those who are single, widowed, and divorced. It is striking that from the age of forty-five, the percentage of women without spouses (56·7 per cent) is almost exactly four times as great as that of men without spouses (14·5 per cent). Many of the men in this age-group probably had wives below the age of 45.

Co-residential polygyny is obviously very rare. It was non-existent in Tanjong, and there were only two cases of it (each man maintaining two wives) in the Municipal sample. In both instances the men were indigenous Malays and were educated in English as well as in the vernacular. One was a clerk and the other an accountant, thus confirming the Malays' own assertion that usually only men in the higher income levels can afford to be polygynous.

Households of extended families, where three generations (a grand-parent, parent, and child) are resident, are remarkably few in number. In Tanjong they were three out of 48 households, or 6·3 per cent. In the

[1] p. 61.

Municipality they were a total of 42 out of 572 households, or 7·3 per cent.[1]

SUMMARY

In both the rural and urban areas, the most common household type is indubitably the simple family. Single-person 'households' are concentrated in the Municipality because in the majority of cases the individuals concerned are immigrants who came to the Colony in order to seek employment, and obviously they have more opportunity for success in the town than in the country. Co-residential polygyny is exceptional in the Municipality and non-existent in Tanjong. Other variations in household composition between rural and urban communities appear to be primarily functions of occupational structure and of housing shortage in the Municipality. Finally, among both groups, it is comparatively rare to find in the same household kinsmen who stand in more distant relationships to one other member than that of siblings or parent-child.

Some observations are necessary here with reference to the effect of divorce on household composition. The ease and frequency of divorce[2] are in large part responsible for the fact that young children do not always live with both parents, and that middle-aged women who are abandoned by their husbands have to join permanently the home of a married child or of a sibling as dependent relatives. Younger divorcées who on account of their youth or greater attractiveness have more possibilities of re-marriage may live with their relatives only temporarily. All this means that household groupings generally lack enduring stability. The only assertion that one can safely make about household composition is that it is rare for a Singapore Malay woman to live apart from her own young unmarried children. Although the various schools of Islam give the father the prior right to the custody of his children when they are past early childhood, Malay custom shows preference for the mother in this respect. Cases of disputes between parents concerning their children's custody were comparatively rare in 1949 and 1950, and the practice as well as the customary rule was for young and unmarried children to follow their mother.

---

[1] In Kelantan, Rosemary Firth found that 57 out of 331 (17·2 per cent) households were of the extended family type as here defined. Op. cit., pp. 6-7.

[2] See below, ch. 6.

4

Marriage

MALAYS conduct their marriages according to the principles of Islam. Proof that a union has been solemnized is readily obtained from an examination of the marriage registers for Muslims in the Colony.

Permanent *liaisons* with cohabitation were extremely rare among Singapore Malays. There was some extra-marital intercourse, but it was usually surreptitious. One almost never found a Malay couple living together as man and wife under the same roof for several months or years without having gone through the Muslim form of marriage. This was so partly on account of the fact that divorces were easily obtainable. Marriage was not treated as a sacred tie, but primarily as a contract,[1] and people entered into it with the knowledge that if one formed an affection for some other person the present union could be dissolved in order to embark upon another with the new love. For a Muslim man, divorce is little more than a formality and he can obtain it at will. Moreover, he may have up to four wives simultaneously. For a woman it is extremely difficult in theory to obtain a divorce if her husband is unwilling to grant her one. However, Malay men considered it contemptible to hold a wife against her will, and a husband who was reluctant or slow to pronounce the divorce formula was goaded into doing so by his wife shaming and insulting him in public.

Another factor against permanent *liaisons* was that the community viewed with horror the couple (especially the woman) who cohabited without being legally married, and a woman who was bold enough to do so, just to 'follow' a man, *ikut sahaja*, was severely condemned and ostracized. Pressure was constantly brought to bear upon the couple to separate if there was a serious impediment to contracting marriage.

LEGAL ASPECTS

The general principle regarding the marriage and divorce procedures of the Muslim population of Singapore was that these institutions must be regulated according to Muslim law. Provision was made for this in Vol. 2 of *The Laws of the Straits Settlements* (1936 edition). Chapter 57 is entitled 'The Mohammedans Ordinance'.

[1] It is customary, however, for Muslim prayers and blessings to be intoned before the contract of marriage is signed.

According to Muslim law a Muslim man may marry, apart from a Muslim woman, a Christian or a Jewess. He may not marry an idolatress. He may be married to no more than four women simultaneously. A Muslim woman, on the other hand, can marry only a Muslim and can have only one husband at a time. A man may not marry his mother, grandmother, daughter, granddaughter, sister, parent's sibling or sibling's child; his present wife's mother, grandmother, daughter, granddaughter, sister; his parent's sister or sibling's daughter ; a woman related to him in any of these degrees through fosterage ; a widow or divorced wife of his father, grandfather, son or grandson.

A Muslim woman must have a legal guardian, a *wali*, to give her away in marriage. She cannot give herself or anyone else in marriage. The *wali* is her father, or in the event of his being dead, her closest adult agnate. If the *wali* is unable to be present at the signing of the marriage contract he can officially delegate a *wakil*, or agent, to act in his place. It is the duty of a *wali* to arrange for a suitable marriage for his ward when she has reached puberty. If a woman has no living *wali*, or if her *wali* persistently puts difficulties in the way of finding her a husband, she has the right to appeal to a *kathi*. The latter may then assume towards her the position of *wali*: a traditional Saying of the Prophet is that 'To her that has no *wali*, the civil authority is *wali*.'[1]

Section 10 of the Mohammedans Ordinance made the registration of every marriage, divorce, or revocation of divorce compulsory; and only a *kathi* or the Registrar of Mohammedan Marriages could issue a certificate of marriage, divorce or revocation of divorce. In contrast to law and practice in the Malay States, *kathi* in Singapore received no remuneration from Government.

The marriage contract was signed by the bride's legal guardian and by the groom in the presence of male witnesses and of the *kathi*. The bride herself was not required to sign the register, but she could do so if she wished. The *kathi* had to give one copy of the marriage certificate to the bride and one to the groom. According to Muslim law, a girl's marriage contract can be signed irrespective of her age, but consummation must wait until she has reached puberty. The Colony's law, therefore, allowed *kathi* to register the marriage of a girl who was under the age of fifteen.

The effect of marriage on property was dealt with in Part III of the Ordinance. A Muslim woman in the Colony had an absolute right over all the property acquired by her previous to her marriage and could dispose of it by will, by deed or otherwise, with or without the concurrence of her husband. She had also the same rights over any property acquired by her during marriage if such acquisition was the result of inheritance, legacy or gift, or of wages and earnings gained by her in any employment or trade carried on by her and not by her husband. She could sue in her own name and was liable on her own contracts.

[1] See R. J. Wilkinson, *Law*, p. 53.

CHOICE OF PARTNERS

Only about one per cent of Malays remained unmarried throughout life.[1] A sharp difference was drawn by the Malays themselves between the marriage of a virgin girl (*anak dara*) and that of a *janda*. A *janda* is a divorcée or widow, a woman who has been, but no longer is, married. The status of the groom also had some importance and one ascertained whether he was a *bujang sĕkali*[2] (a man who had never been married before), or whether he was divorced, widowed, or a married man entering into a polygynous union. The most elaborate pomp, other things being equal, took place on the occasion of a wedding between an *anak dara* and a *bujang sĕkali*.

Preference was given to marriage within one's cultural, linguistic, territorial and income group. Further, preference was given to marriage within the group of kindred. Parents wished their children to marry within the same village, or to have a spouse from a neighbouring district; or failing that, within the Island of Singapore. This objection was sometimes extended to a man who resided in the Island but whose native home was elsewhere. Thus parents might refuse a suitor born in Pahang or Selangor or Kelantan who had a job in Singapore and undertook to continue living in the Colony: a Malay's link with his home town is known to be very strong and the girl's parents feared that one day he might give up his job and decide to visit his relatives for an unspecified period of time, taking his wife and children with him. This type of behaviour was by no means infrequent, and often a Singapore woman asked to be divorced rather than to be separated from her own kinsfolk.

Again, preference was given to a marriage linking two elementary families with similar types of income and standards of living. The chief yardstick for measuring the economic status of the bride was the occupation of her father or, if the latter was dead, of the brother or close kinsman who supported the household. Usually the daughter of a rubber-tapper married a rubber-tapper, a domestic servant, or a semi-skilled labourer. She might marry an office boy or a policeman but it was unlikely that she would marry a clerk or a schoolteacher.

Marriage within the kinship group was always sought. Again and again one heard Malays emphatically commenting about a prospective marriage partner in a definite tone of approval, *dia bukan orang lain* (he, or she, is not a stranger). On the other hand, certain unions between relatives are banned either by Islam, or by custom, or by both. The Muslim law regarding prohibited degrees has been stated, and there is also an *adat* ban on those unions. Moreover, there is an *adat* ban on certain unions considered permissible by Islam. Such, for instance, is the strong traditional

---

[1] See Census Report for 1947, p. 64.

[2] The word *bujang* has a wider application in the Federation where it is used to refer to both men and women who are single, widowed or divorced. Wilkinson's Dictionary gives all these meanings for *bujang*.

ban against a union of the children of two brothers,[1] and breaches of this ban were few in Singapore. The most frequent explanation for the ban was that such marriages invariably led to family quarrels and divorce. Some said, 'One does not know why this is so, it is perhaps strange, but we Malays have always found that when the children of two brothers marry, disaster follows in the shape of divorce or of dire poverty or of the early death of one of the spouses. Of course such a union is *ṣah* (permissible by religion), but since it has been shown for generations and generations to lead to havoc, we have a strong *adat* ban against it.' Others tried to explain the ban in rational terms. 'Any small quarrel between husband and wife, when they are the children of two brothers, tends to become magnified because each brother naturally takes the side of his child. When men are brothers, they speak to one another with little restraint and then you have not only the breakdown of a marriage but also a serious split between brothers. On the other hand, if it is the children of a sister and brother who marry, or of two sisters, there is little risk to run as, in the first case a sister will not venture to argue violently with her brother, and in the second case two sisters rarely quarrel bitterly about each other's children; even if they did so, the quarrel is unlikely to be as serious as a quarrel between men.'

When such explanations were propounded I often asked, 'What happens then if one brother is dead, or both?' The reply varied. Sometimes I was told that if one brother was dead and the other had become the legal guardian (*wali*) of his orphaned niece, the marriage of the two cousins would give the *wali* excessive power over the bride. At other times the informant fell back upon the more common argument that simply because they were the children of two brothers, the marriage would bring ill fate to the parties irrespective of any other considerations. At this point attention was usually drawn to a concrete case of a disastrous union of this type.

In an earlier Chapter I mentioned the fact that first cousins of all types (*sa-pupu*) felt almost as closely related to each other as full siblings and that they often referred to each other simply as *abang* (older brother), *kakak* (older sister) or *adik* (younger sibling). It is therefore interesting to note in this context that sometimes Singapore Malays logically extended the ban to the children of two male first cousins. It was irrelevant whether the fathers were themselves the children of two brothers, or of two sisters, or of a brother and a sister. The significant point was that they were men linked by blood almost as closely as brothers.

There was, further, an *adat* ban on inter-generation marriage when the kinship tie was close (i.e., within the range of the *saudara děkat*), irrelevantly of the actual ages of the parties. This was the theory. In practice, however, people much more easily forgave the marriage of a girl to a man senior to her in generation status than they did that of a man to a woman of senior generation. They explained that since a man should enjoy a status

[1] cf. H. Subandrio who states that, in Java, 'marriage between descendants of two brothers is not considered desirable', op. cit., p. 64.

superior to that of his wife, he would be in a very embarrassing position if
he married a woman whom he had previously addressed with some respect
as 'aunt' (*ĕmak chik*). In 1949 and 1950 inter-generation marriages did
occur without raising much more than murmurs of disapproval in the
community, but I was told that twenty or thirty years earlier they would
not have been permitted. Further, it must be noted that inter-generation
marriages were rarely first marriages for both parties; first marriages were
almost exclusively arranged by the couple's parents who exercised great
care to ensure that no customary rule was infringed.

The Javanese immigrants were particularly strict in these matters of rank
and status within the kin group and their *adat* prohibited some types of
first cousin unions which were fully permissible among the local Malays.
Briefly stated, the Javanese rule was that, given a group of siblings, the
son of the eldest could marry any of his female cousins, but the son of the
youngest sibling could not marry any of these girls; similarly the son of the
second older sibling might marry any of his female cousins with the exception of the daughters of the eldest sibling of his parent. The age of the
cousins themselves was immaterial in this context; it was their rank alone
which was of importance, and this rank followed the order of birth of their
respective parents.[1] Although many informants stated that since the war
less attention was being paid in Singapore to this particular rule, I noted
that breaches seemed rare and that when they occurred they gave rise to
much scandalized gossip.

I said that marriage within the group of kindred was always sought.
Consequently when a girl reached marriageable age, it was usual for the
parents of eligible young kinsmen to consider the match. Whenever practicable, she was married off to a *saudara*. If the girl's parents were first
approached on behalf of an *orang lain*, they acquainted their kinsmen of the
offer at once, taking especial care to inform the *saudara* who had young sons
in order to give them first choice. Sometimes if the girl's parents desired a
particular kinsman to be her husband, they refused proposals from strangers
without hesitation and waited for a year or two until the man of their
choice acquired a suitable job or became a more skilled workman in his
trade, or until he and his parents had accumulated some capital. But if
after this period no proposal came from this kinsman or from any other
suitable kinsman, the parents with a free conscience accepted offers from
strangers. It was common then for them to precede their news of the
proposed engagement with the statement, 'We have waited a long time,
but since you do not seem to want her for your son, we are considering a
match with another young man.'

In many other Muslim societies, such as in Egypt, Palestine, Morocco,
and Arabia, it is the son of the father's brother who has the prior claim.
Indeed, in Artas, the Palestinian village H. Granqvist studied, this claim
had a quasi-legal character, for if the man did not get his *bint 'amm*

---

[1] cf. above, p. 28

(father's brother's daughter), 'the bridegroom through whom he loses his bride must give him a certain compensation.'[1] The author cites the case of one thwarted cousin receiving £10. Among Singapore Malays, however, no specific kinsman had the prior right to a girl's hand in marriage while, as has been shown, marriage between the children of two brothers was particularly avoided. Cross-cousins, children of two sisters, *dua-pupu* (except children of two male first cousins), and *tiga-pupu* were considered equally suitable partners. Affines were preferred to total strangers. But no one kinsman had such automatic claims upon a girl that her parents or another suitor must pay him compensation for depriving him of her.

Age. Ideally, for a first marriage for both parties the difference in age should be small, the groom being older than his bride by two to five years. This was often so in point of fact.[2] It was considered preferable for a girl to marry within two or three years of her having reached puberty, but often the event was postponed until she was eighteen or nineteen years old. A Singapore Malay girl rarely remained unmarried at twenty. Contrary to popular belief about the connection between a tropical climate and early maturation, Malay girls do not reach puberty earlier than European girls. Thirteen is said to be slightly premature for puberty; the norm appears to be more in the vicinity of fourteen years of age, and it is not unknown for girls to reach puberty only at fifteen.[3]

Most Malay girls in Singapore married when they were between sixteen and nineteen years of age, while the grooms were between nineteen and twenty-three years old when they first married.

I have already stated that in accordance with Islam the law in the Colony allowed *kathi* to register the marriage of a Muslim girl who had not yet reached puberty, but that the consummation of the union could not take place until she became physically mature. While it was very rare for local Malay parents to sign a marriage contract when their daughters were still in childhood, the practice was less uncommon among the Javanese and Boyanese in Singapore. In the latter case, the bride continued to live at her parental home until she reached puberty, when she was formally handed over to her husband for the consummation. Such an arrangement was known as *nikah gantong* (suspended marriage contract) and might perhaps be described as an irrevocable engagement to marry, for the engagement could be broken only by a divorce.

Local Malay parents did not like a younger daughter to marry before her older sister, but they had no objection to a girl marrying before her older brother. When a girl married before her *kakak*, her groom was said to

---

[1] H. Granqvist, *Marriage Conditions in a Palestinian Village*, 2 vols., Helsingfors; vol. 1, 1931; vol. 2, 1935; vol. 1, p. 71.

[2] It is not possible to substantiate this from the Registers of Marriage, as the age of the groom is not entered, only that of the bride; therefore I am basing the statement on information personally gathered.

[3] I was able to check the ages of many young girls in the areas where I lived from their birth certificates.

mĕlangkah batang (lit., stride across a rod). This usually occurred if the older girl was an invalid or of immoral reputation, or presented some other serious impediment to marriage; the groom gave her a complete suit of clothes as a free and unconditional gift.[1] The Javanese in Singapore had the same custom, but they also extended it to cover an older unmarried brother of the bride. However, the Javanese like the local Malays showed no objection in theory or in practice to a girl marrying before her older brother.

Consent. A firmly established principle was that an *anak dara*'s opinion, let alone consent, need not be sought when her marriage was contemplated. All the preliminary negotiations took place when she was not present and indeed even when the match was decided her parents did not inform her. Usually it was left to her sisters or young friends to give her the news. However reluctant the *anak dara* might be, either to the idea of marriage in general or to that of marriage with the particular man her parents had selected, she did not utter a word of protest. To do so was considered not only highly improper but plainly indecent. Her only resistance to the match could take place *after* the wedding ceremonies were over, and that was by refusing to consummate the marriage. When a foreign observer pointed out to Singapore Malay parents that such a custom appeared to victimize the bride, the usual reply was: 'But among Malays an *anak dara* cannot speak when her parents have taken such a decision; she just cannot; she is too shy. Besides, what opinion can she have on the matter? She is still a child; she has no experience and her parents love her and choose the best husband they can for her.'

As for the groom's consent, a young man had some small freedom of choice. He at least was consulted and if he refused outright, the idea of the match was abandoned. Usually, parents instructed a relative to approach their son and ask him whether he was willing to consider marriage at all. If he said that the prospect did not alarm him—very few young men were reluctant—the name of the girl was disclosed to him if he knew her. Otherwise she was described to him as pretty, or as a good housekeeper or simply as eminently suitable; sometimes it might even be arranged for him to catch a glimpse of her or to see a photograph. On the other hand, if the young man had already been attracted by an *anak dara* whom his parents approved of, then again through intermediaries he hinted that he would be particularly happy to marry *her*. Generally, however, it was common for a first marriage to take place after the minimum amount of consultation with the groom. It must be remembered that young Singapore Malays were usually unable to raise the amount of the wedding expenses and usually depended upon their parents to do so.

Furthermore, even if he had savings and however good his earning

---

[1] There is a similar practice among the Melanau. Morris states that when gifts are made to a bride, 'a gift must be made to her elder sister if the latter is still unmarried'. H. S. Morris, op. cit., p. 132.

ability, a young man needed the support of his close kin for his marriage negotiations to succeed. In the case of a first marriage especially, few parents would give their daughter to a man whose parents disagreed with his choice. Agreement between both sets of parents was a *sine qua non*, even when the groom was financially independent and ready to join his bride's household or to provide her with a separate home. Although among Singapore Malays *besan* (two pairs of parents whose children have married) did not enter into close social relationships, and although it was extremely rare for a bride to live with her parents-in-law and so on the face of it the groom's *saudara* would have little authority over the bride, there was a strong tradition that a first marriage must have the blessing of the groom's as well as of the bride's relatives. The groom, his parents and close kinsmen were, for these purposes, treated as a solidary group, whatever internal disagreement there might be among them. His kinsmen's opposition to the match was taken as a serious insult to the girl and her kin, who in turn therefore refused their consent. Moreover, the girl's parents feared that after the union the young husband might show little reluctance to divorce her on the flimsiest pretext because he would be influenced by criticisms of his bride before and after the marriage.

So far we have looked upon the choice of marriage partners from the point of view of their social personalities, as members of a particular group. However, another factor was also considered important by Malays, and that was the purely individual or personal character of the bride and groom. Necessary attributes for the former were that she be chaste, a diligent and cheerful housekeeper, and happy to stay at home. A young man, on the other hand, should above all be industrious, have a sense of financial responsibility and also, if possible, be good-natured. As for physical attributes, it was much more important for the bride to be good-looking than it was for the groom. The principal elements of beauty for a woman were a somewhat fairer than average complexion and a slender figure. A fair complexion was also highly valued in a man.

CEREMONIAL PROCEDURE

There were five main stages: proposal, formal engagement, wedding ceremonies, consummation, and formal visiting by the pair.

The proposal was usually made by a friend or kinsman of the groom who was already acquainted with the girl's parents. Usually a middle-aged or elderly woman was selected, and she received no material reward for her services. There were no professional go-betweens in Singapore Malay society. The woman approached the mother of the girl, using one of several conventional phrases. She might say, 'What beautiful flowers you have in your garden, especially this one. Please tell me whether it is already promised to anybody, for if not I would dearly love to have it.' Or else, 'I have an empty cage and you, on the other hand, have a lovely bird. Would you let me have it for my cage? It will be treasured.' Or again, 'I have a male

F

bird languishing because it is lonely. You have a delightful female bird, and why should the two not be united? Otherwise mine may die of solitude.'

If she was willing to consider the match, the girl's mother usually asked for about a week to consult with her husband and close kin, after expressing profuse formal thanks for the proposal. However, if she had no doubts about the undesirability of the union she replied with very great humility that her flower (or bird) was a poor and miserable specimen, which was anyway already promised to someone else. She added that she was, nevertheless, overwhelmed with gratitude at the honour done her and her people by the offer, of which her daughter was totally unworthy. A proposal of marriage was rarely refused in any but this humble way. It was feared that the suitor or his parents, if openly snubbed, might seek revenge by causing a spell to be cast on the girl to make her ill or insane or condemn her to remain an old maid until her death.

Let us assume the girl's mother has agreed to give an answer in a week. The go-between will have described the groom's occupation and income and hinted at the sum of the *bĕlanja kahwin* (wedding expenses) to be paid by the man. The girl's mother then consults with her husband, her older married children and any respected kinsmen of the household. If general opinion is in favour of the match the decision is conveyed to the go-between; the parents of the man are then immediately informed and the day of the formal engagement is fixed upon. On that day older relatives of the suitor (both men and women) formally go to the girl's house. This is called *hantar tanda* (sending the proof) or *hantar chinchin* (sending the ring). The women are received by the female relatives of the bride-to-be, to whom they hand over a gold ring, ornamented trays of flowers and sireh leaves, and often also material for a complete suit of clothes and half the agreed amount of the marriage expenses. (This sum is given in advance in order to enable the girl's parents to start upon the preparations for the wedding.) Their chief representative makes a small speech when presenting the offerings. The period of engagement is formally declared; it is always short—between two and four months. The chief representative of the bride in turn makes a speech of grateful acceptance of the gifts. In another room the men of both parties gather, chant a Muslim prayer and state the terms of the marriage: the full amount of the *bĕlanja kahwin*, of the gifts given, the date of the wedding and the consequences of a breach of promise on either side. The tradition is that should the man decide after the *hantar chinchin* ceremony that he does not wish to go on with the marriage, he forfeits all the gifts he made on that occasion. Should the girl break off the match, she must return all the gifts.

Sometimes on the day of the *hantar chinchin*, mention is also made of the nature of the gifts which the man shall send every month to his bride-to-be —material for clothes, or money, or both. Monthly gifts are in no circumstances returnable if the marriage does not take place. It is extremely rare for any of the conditions to be written down; they are considered sufficiently binding on account of the fact that they have been stated formally by responsible people in the presence of witnesses.[1] Occasionally on that day a decision is made as to where and with whom the couple shall live during the first few months of the marriage.

Whether the couple knew each other or not, it was unusual, once the *hantar tanda* ceremony had taken place, for them to meet face to face until after the contract of marriage was signed. Where they lived in the same village or district, great care was taken by the girl's parents to keep her hidden in the house, thereby showing proper shyness and chastity. In any case, however, once a girl had been formally engaged to marry she was bound to be very strictly limited in her movements as she was held in trust by her parents who frequently observed, 'She is no longer ours'.

Cases of breach of promise were rare and caused such scandal that both parties usually preferred to go through the wedding ceremonies and later arrange a divorce.

The wedding ceremonies proper start with the *nikah* or signing of the marriage contract. This takes place according to Muslim rites and if possible on a Thursday evening, as the eve of Friday (*malam Jumaat*) is considered most auspicious. The groom, suitably escorted, arrives at the house of the bride where he is ushered into a room full of the bride's male kinsmen and guests. The latter, led by the *kathi*, have been chanting Muslim religious verses for some time. When the groom enters, he sits down on a mat facing the *kathi* who holds his hand and asks him to pronounce the set formula of marriage. Then both he and the bride's father or legal guardian sign the marriage register. Legally the pair are married even though they may not yet have met.

Meanwhile, female representatives of the groom have come into the women's room, carrying a gold ring, material for a complete suit of clothes, slippers, head scarf, ornamented trays of flowers and sireh leaves, and a box containing the total amount of the *bĕlanja*. The ring is the same one as had been given on the *hantar chinchin* ceremony. It often belongs to the groom's mother or sister and is returned in many cases to her after the wedding. The money is frequently borrowed for the day, as usually the original sum has been given in one or two instalments some weeks earlier to the bride's parents to spend on the wedding preparations. The gifts are formally received by a representative of the bride.

After the marriage contract has been signed the groom is led into an adjoining room where the female guests are assembled, and goes to a corner where his bride shyly waits on a chair. He puts his right hand over her head for a brief moment, shakes her right hand and goes back to the men's room.

Later, the bride and groom each in turn sit alone upon the decorated throne (*pĕlamin*) in the bridal house and have the palms of their hands smeared with henna (*inai*) by older and respected guests of the same sex.

[1] Several Malay informants explained to me: *Kita orang Mĕlayu 'sign' mulut sahaja* ('We Malays sign with the mouth only.')

If the wedding is on a lavish scale, the henna ceremony takes place again on the following night, the first night being referred to as *malam inai kĕchik*, the small henna night, and the second night as *malam inai bĕsar*, or the great henna night. Again, the bride and groom go through the ceremony separately in the presence of all the female guests. Throughout the procedure the male and female guests stay in different rooms and partake of refreshments separately. The *inai* ceremony always takes place in the women's room where the throne is erected, and when the elderly men come to apply henna to the groom's palms, they enter the room self-consciously, one by one. On henna nights no elaborate meal is served, only tea and sweetmeats. The large feast is served immediately before the *bĕrsanding*. It usually consists of rice cooked in fat (*nasi minyak*), goat's meat or chicken, curried vegetables, pickles and fresh fruit. The *bĕrsanding* is the climax of the wedding, it takes place on the day following the henna ceremonies, and the term refers to the period when the couple finally come to sit together in state on the *pĕlamin* in the presence of the guests; the women sitting on mats on the floor and the men watching just outside the room, from the doors and windows. The most elaborate dress and jewelry are kept for this occasion. This is the moment of the couple's great glory, when they sit enthroned like king and queen for all to gaze upon them, and theoretically[1] it happens only once in the lifetime of a woman, on the occasion of her first marriage. A long piece of cloth is then placed on the ground as a carpet, leading from the throne to two decorated chairs at the other end of the room. The groom gets up, takes his bride by the hand and the pair walk to the chairs and sit on them, while one or two old women are sought and made to sing and dance ludicrously in order to entertain the company. This marks the end of the *bĕrsanding* ceremony and guests begin to depart. As they go, each of them is presented with *bunga tĕlor*, a coloured hard-boiled egg fixed with a wire on to a small triangular packet of yellow glutinous rice. A coloured paper flower is arranged at the top of the wire. When the room is empty save for close relatives, a tray of food is brought with rice, cooked meat and vegetables, pickles, and tea or syrup. The bride and groom have meanwhile removed their heavy clothes and ornaments and changed into clean and neat ordinary dress. The bride then sits on a mat on the floor near her groom and serves food to him for the first time. She is earnestly urged by the company to help herself to some food as well and eat, but she is not expected to do so. Instead she keeps quiet, eyes averted, and waits for her husband to clear his plate so that she can give him a second helping.

The groom goes back to sleep in his own house on that night. The following morning there is a gay ceremony known as *mandi mandi* (bathing) when the couple sit together, enveloped in one sarong, and are ceremonially bathed by old female friends. There is great mirth shown and everybody present gets wet in the process as the women who pour the water on

[1] See below, p. 79.

the couple consider it their duty to sprinkle the guests generously as well. From this day the groom can sleep in the house of his bride, although consummation does not take place immediately. Two or three days after the *mandi mandi* the couple, suitably escorted, go to the house of the groom's parents where another throne awaits them upon which they sit in state again, but only for a very brief while. If the house is some distance away from that of the bride, they may stay the night. Otherwise they return to the bride's home the same day. Whatever the future residence of the couple, the first few days after marriage are always spent at the bride's home.

There was great preference for the *bĕrsanding* to take place when there was a full moon, in the middle of the Muslim month, which is of course lunar. Some Muslim months were considered particularly auspicious for weddings: *Zol Hijah*, *Rabi' Awal*, and *Jamadil Akhir*. On the other hand, the month of the fast, *Ramadan*, was generally declared to be most unsuitable for a wedding. Figures from the Registers of Muslim Marriages (each entry bears the Muslim as well as the Western calendar date) confirm this. Over a period of twenty years (1929-49), the number of marriages was highest for a Muslim year in the above-named three months, with *Zol Hijah* usually leading, and lowest in *Ramadan*.[1]

Consummation usually took place within about ten days of the *bĕrsanding*. It was traditional for the bride to put up a show of resistance, and for the groom to use no great physical force to persuade her to submit.[2] The bride's mother was greatly shamed if the girl gave in too readily, for this showed her to be badly brought up and singularly lacking in chastity. It was common for women to boast of, or exaggerate, the duration of the period during which they or their daughters rejected a husband's advances. When a decent interval of about ten days had elapsed, some parents forced the issue by leaving the couple alone in the house and locking them in. Sometimes, however, the resistance put up by the bride was quite genuine and so prolonged that the marriage, without its ever being consummated, ended in divorce. This was the traditional way in which a girl could forcefully express her disapproval of the match arranged by her parents. Many young brides remained adamant and neither magical potions, nor physical punishment by their parents, nor advice, prevailed. The groom was then entitled to be compensated by the bride's parents who must refund him double the amount of the *bĕlanja kahwin* he gave them, and return the gold ring and other gifts he made on the day of the *nikah*. Most grooms, however, were content to accept just the amount of the *bĕlanja*. Even this the bride's parents could not usually provide, as the money had already been

---

[1] Among the Achehnese the months of *Rabi' Awal*, *Rabi'al-Akhir* and *Sha'ban* were regarded as lucky months for marriage, according to C. Snouck Hurgronje, *The Achehnese*, translated by A. W. S. O'Sullivan, 2 vols., Leyden 1906, vol. 1, p. 303. In one area in Java in 1954 I found that people favoured the month of *Zol Hijah* for the major wedding ceremonies.

[2] This was also the custom among the Achehnese. See Hurgronje, op. cit., vol. 1, p. 325.

spent on the wedding ceremonies. The case was then taken to the *kathi* for arbitration.

After the consummation of the marriage the bridal pair went on ceremonial visits to the homes of their older relatives and respected friends. Usually, one or two middle-aged kinswomen of the bride or of the groom accompanied them, and notice of the visit was given in advance to the persons concerned so that they could prepare refreshments for the couple and for their escort. It was also customary for the bride and groom to be given a small gift by their hosts on such occasions, either money, or a length of cloth.

So far I have spoken only of the case of a first marriage for both parties, when such a union took place according to the ideal practice of the community. It must not be believed, however, that all first marriages occurred in the manner described. It did happen, sometimes, that an *anak dara* seriously compromised her reputation by having pre-marital sexual relations. In such circumstances pressure was exerted on the seducer to marry her—he was rarely unwilling—and a very hasty ceremony was arranged. The groom was expected to give only a minimum amount of *bĕlanja kahwin*, often $50 or less. There was no *hantar chinchin* ceremony and no *malam inai*. The whole bridal ceremonial was contracted to the few minutes it takes the *kathi* to recite the appropriate prayers and prepare the entries for the marriage register. *Bĕrsanding* did not normally occur on such occasions either. No proper feast was prepared; only a sweet broth of dried beans (*bubor kachang*) was served to the few witnesses or guests present. The shame of having been married in this summary manner always pursued a woman. People muttered several years after the event, 'So-and-so, well she behaves properly now, but do you think she had a proper wedding? Not at all, it was just a matter of serving *bubor kachang*.'

There were also a few rare cases of a couple eloping together and seeking marriage before the *kathi* for a different district in the Colony. Generally, however, when an affair was suspected between two young people a *bubor kachang* marriage was arranged in the village of the couple, or of the girl if they came from different areas, rather than risk the even greater shame of the couple running away to get married somewhere else.

Marriage of Janda.

So far we have considered the marriage of an *anak dara* with a *bujang sĕkali*. Other possible unions are between an *anak dara* and a man who has been previously married; between a *janda* and a *bujang sĕkali*; and between a *janda* and a man previously married.

In the first case, that of a union between an *anak dara* and a man who has been previously married, the same care was generally taken about the marriage arrangements as obtained when it was a first marriage for both parties, and ceremonies were usually on as elaborate a scale. When a wedding was discussed, the marital status of the bride, not that of the groom, was the chief consideration. The distinction was primarily between an *anak dara* wedding and a *janda* wedding, the former being recognized as an occasion for more pomp and rejoicing than the latter. A widower or divorced man could and did sit in state, *bĕrsanding*, when he married an *anak dara* (although this *bĕrsanding* was not considered as of quite the same order as that of a couple being married both for the first time). It was deemed suitable for *janda* to marry men who were either widowed or divorced. If a *bujang sĕkali* were to marry a *janda* he would forgo the valued privilege of sitting in state with his bride on the occasion of his first wedding. Sometimes, however, if the *janda* was very young (in her late teens or early twenties) and had no children, a *bĕrsanding* on a somewhat modest scale was arranged. It would be difficult to over-estimate the importance which both men and women attached to this ceremonial. The few minutes during which the couple sat enthroned were their greatest glory: again and again Malays stressed that the couple were like a king and queen (*macham raja*) during those minutes.

Preferential forms of marriage for a *janda* were the same as for an *anak dara*, except that less careful attention was given to the planning of the second marriage by her legal guardian. For instance, there was less resistance shown by her relatives if a local Malay *janda* married an immigrant Malay than there would have been if the bride were still an *anak dara*. Also, a *janda* frequently married a man who was her senior by ten or more years, whereas the discrepancy between the ages of an *anak dara* bride and her groom was rarely as great.

As far as consent was concerned, in accordance with Muslim law and Malay custom a *janda* was consulted regarding any proposed match, and if she was unwilling the union rarely took place: her first marriage had emancipated her. However, there were sometimes very young *janda* for whom their guardians arranged a second marriage without consultation.

Whereas the wedding ceremonies of an *anak dara* usually continued over a period of two or three days, those of a *janda* lasted only one morning or afternoon. After the *nikah* a small meal was served to the few guests present. As in the case of an *anak dara*, however, the groom lived in his bride's home for at least a few days after the wedding. Consummation usually took place within a day or two of the ceremony; it was unnecessary for a *janda* to show great resistance, although this sometimes happened. Ceremonial visiting of older relatives and close friends also took place a few days after the wedding of a *janda*.

With a *janda* as with an *anak dara*, if the wedding had been hastily arranged after an elopement, or because there had been an illicit union between the pair which gave rise to scandal, the only feasting was that of *bubor kachang*.

RESIDENCE AFTER MARRIAGE

We know that it was the custom for the bridal pair to spend at least the first few days, (usually the first few weeks) at the home of the bride's parents.[1] Whenever practicable they continued to live there until after the birth of their first child. Then they often built, or rented, a small house for themselves, preferably in close proximity to that of the wife's parents. In town, they rented a room. The nature of the man's job was the most important single factor in the situation. Should both parties come from fishing villages, the young man could easily move to his wife's home and continue to carry on his own occupation there, after some preliminary arrangements regarding the partners with whom he would go out to sea. If, on the other hand, he was a soldier, or a policeman, he and his wife were usually given housing by his employers.

In the case of the husband going to live permanently in his wife's village, every year or so the couple together with any children of the union went to spend a few weeks in his native district. If the man insisted on settling there, his wife almost inevitably raised serious objections to the proposal, and often disagreement on such an issue precipitated a divorce. This is one reason why preference was usually given to marriage with a fellow-villager, and many young women have told me: 'It is better to marry within one's own village even if the man is poor than to take a rich husband from another area. What is the use of having a belly filled with food if the heart is sad? With a fellow-villager you are sure of staying close to your own people in your own locality; with a stranger, whatever his promises, he will soon want to take you along to his own district and then quarrels will start.'

There were several occasions on which a young woman who had left to settle elsewhere with her husband was expected back at her own parental home:

1. on *hari raya* (the feast after the end of the fast) which has the same sentimental connotations for Malays as Christmas has for the English;
2. when she had reached the last stages of pregnancy, so that her mother might look after her and the baby[2];
3. when either she or one of her children was seriously ill.

Whenever possible the husband also came to live in his wife's parental home during these periods. Moreover, if he was in a job which entitled him to paid annual leave, it was expected that with his wife and children he would spend most of the period in his parents-in-law's home.

In the census I took of Tanjong in 1949, out of 32 married couples there were 12 in which both husband and wife were natives of Tanjong. Among the remaining 20 couples there were two instances where both

---

[1] cf. R. O. Winstedt, *The Malay Magician*, London 1951, p. 121; 'Everywhere it is usual for the husband to live in his bride's home for some while after the marriage.'

[2] If the woman already had a large family and found it inconvenient to take them all with her to her mother's house, the mother might come to the daughter's home to look after her.

partners had settled in the village from elsewhere; only four wives had left their native homes to follow their spouse in Tanjong, while fourteen husbands had done so. The figures therefore confirm the generally expressed preferences for matrilocality as second best after marriage within the same village.

ECONOMIC ASPECTS

Among Singapore Malays there was nearly always a nett deficit incurred both by the bride's and the groom's close kinsmen at the end of the wedding ceremonies, when the accounts were finally balanced.

At a marriage with an *anak dara* it was the duty of the groom or of his parents to provide the following:

1. *Bĕlanja kahwin* (wedding expenses). The amount usually varied between $101 and $301.
2. Gifts for the bride during the period of engagement. $15 to $50.
3. *Mas kahwin* traditionally fixed at $22.50. (Payment of this sum could be, and often was, deferred.) *Mas kahwin* is also known as *mahr*.
4. Feasts at the groom's own home for his own guests during the wedding ceremonies. $30 to $60.
5. A reception at his parents' home for the bride when he brought her there formally for the first time. $20 to $40.
6. His wedding clothes. $15 to $40.

The bride's parents, on the other hand, had to supply:

1. The bridal bed. $25 to $40.
2. An ornamental throne (*pĕlamin*) for the couple to sit in state at the climax of the wedding ceremonies. $10 to $30.
3. Wedding feasts for the guests. $100 to $300.
4. The bride's apparel. $15 to $60.
5. Music and dancing (a *ronggeng* troupe). $25 to $50. This was not essential, and was provided only when the bride's parents could afford the additional expense.
6. Gift to the *kathi*. $15 to $30.

The above were the major items of expenditure. There were, in addition, smaller items such as the cost of transport to invite personally most of the wedding guests—or for 'modern' Malays the cost of printing and posting wedding invitations.

On the *credit* side of the budget were the gifts from kinsmen and other guests. Those on the groom's side sent them to the groom's house, and those on the bride's to the bride's. The custom was for the gifts to be sent a few days before the wedding ceremony. Very close relatives, such as married siblings of the bride or groom, parents' siblings, and first cousins, were expected to give either substantial sums of money varying from $10 to $30, or else foodstuffs for the wedding feasts, such as large quantities of rice, sugar, or flour. The amounts varied with the prosperity of the relative concerned. More distant relatives and close friends gave smaller sums, varying between $5 and $10; or some yards of cloth for a *baju* or for a complete suit; or a few pounds of rice, sugar, or flour. As far as gifts from ordinary friends and acquaintances were concerned, there was a clear difference in practice between the local Singapore Malays and the immigrant groups from Java and Bawean. The latter did not partake of the wedding feasts without paying a minimum sum of $2 per adult head, whereas among the local Malays it was not considered necessary for others than relatives and very close friends to give anything at all. In this respect, the local Singapore Malays differed from those of Kelantan whom Firth describes in *Malay Fishermen*. In Kelantan every guest makes a contribution and Firth estimates that an immediate excess of receipts over expenses is common when the final accounts are balanced after the feast.[1]

In Singapore weddings, however, there was nearly always a deficit. This was particularly so in the case of local Malays; and all my immigrant informants assured me that in spite of their guests' contribution only exceptionally did receipts cover expenditure, and never did they exceed it. The amount of the deficit was said to vary for both the bride's and the groom's party from $10 to $200. Frequently, women would remark that they used to own a lot of jewelry, but had to sell most of it to pay for their children's weddings; others spoke of heavy debts incurred.

On the other hand, expenditure for a *janda* wedding was usually on a reduced scale and led to little indebtedness. Only when the *janda* was very young, or still a virgin (on account of the non-consummation of her first marriage), or had well-to-do parents, did large-scale feasting at her wedding occur. Otherwise there was no *hantar chinchin* ceremony, no gifts were made to the bride-to-be during the period of the engagement, and the *bĕlanja kahwin* was usually only $50 in either the rural or the urban areas. About a third of this sum was spent on a bedspread, bed frills and a mosquito net. No elaborate throne was erected. Wedding clothes for the bride and groom were not hired; each might wear the clothes already bought for the previous *hari raya*. Frequently, however, the bride spent about $10 on four or five yards of material which she or her relatives made into a *baju* and sarong.

Whether the bride was an *anak dara* or a *janda*, it was customary for her to go with her groom, about two weeks after the wedding, on formal visits to the homes of their older close relatives and of intimate friends of their parents. Their hosts, as was said earlier, gave the pair a small gift, either money ($2 to $10), or a length of cloth. Often, however, the value of the gifts received on all those occasions barely covered the travelling expenses of the couple and their escort.

POLYGYNY

It was not possible to obtain any official figures as to the extent of Malay

[1] Raymond Firth, *Malay Fishermen*, pp. 177-82.

(or Muslim) polygyny in the Colony, for when a marriage was solemnized and registered the groom was not asked to state whether he already had a wife, and there was no entry in the records at the Registry of Muslim Marriages and Divorces which dealt with this point.[1] According to Islam, of course, a man may be married to not more than four wives at any given time; and he should treat all of them equally well or else abstain from marrying more than one. That is to say, he should show no preference to any one of them in any respect, either in his financial contributions towards their maintenance, or in the demonstration of his affection. On this last score some Malays together with modern Muslims elsewhere argue that the Prophet thereby indirectly banned polygyny, since no man could consistently treat his two (or more) wives with exactly the same amount of love and affection, although it would be simple to provide them with the same amount of material comfort.

In the absence of any figures or estimates of the extent of polygyny in the Colony or the Peninsula, I can only say that it was my impression (as well as that of other observers[2]) that Malay polygynous unions are not frequent. The Social Welfare Department Survey shows that in 572 Malay households only 2 were polygynous.[3] In Tanjong in 1949 and 1950 there was not one instance of polygyny which was known or made public. I specify 'made public', because it is of course possible—though improbable—that one of the married men quietly kept another wife in town or in some other part of the Colony. On the other hand, when I went to live in a large Malay suburb I came to know personally of four cases of polygynous unions. In the last area where I was engaged in field work (an urban district inhabited by labourers, semi-skilled and skilled workers, and some clerks and teachers), there were two polygynous unions. In no instance did a man have more than two wives. Indeed, cases of Malay men married simultaneously to more than two women were unheard of in Singapore, although they were known among members of Malay Royal Houses and among some wealthy landowners or chiefs in the Peninsula.

It is important to distinguish at the outset between formal and active polygyny. By formal polygyny I mean a situation where a man lives with and supports only one wife although he is legally married to another woman as well, whom he neither visits nor maintains. This occurs in the following three sets of circumstances:

1. A man comes to the Colony from a State in the Peninsula or from some part of Indonesia where he leaves a wife. He finds a job and marries again

---

[1] Rosemary Firth, op. cit., found 16 polygynous households in her field of study. She has an interesting section on polygyny in her monograph (pp. 35-42).

[2] See *Adatrechtbundels*, vol. xxvi: *Maleisch Gebied en Borneo*, The Hague 1926, p. 181 quoting from N. B. Dennys, *A Descriptive Dictionary of British Malaya*, London 1894, pp. 304-5, 'polygamy is sanctioned by religion and custom amongst the Malays, but is the exception rather than the rule, not above five to ten per cent indulging in more than one wife.'   [3] See above, p. 58.

in Singapore, settling with his new wife, often without troubling to inform his earlier wife or to remit money to her. She sometimes seeks a divorce on the grounds of desertion and lack of maintenance, but until she obtains it, the man is technically polygynous. Sometimes, though less frequently, this type of situation occurs when all parties are resident in the Colony. For instance, if the deserted first wife is elderly, she may not trouble to seek a divorce since she knows she is unlikely to marry again, and a divorce for desertion and lack of maintenance would cost her money and involve her in several journeys to the *kathi*'s house. Usually, an elderly woman has adult children who are willing to support her.

2. Another situation of formal polygyny occurs when a man decides to take a second wife and share his favours between her and his first wife, but the latter refuses to cohabit with him. So he establishes a separate residence with his new wife, meanwhile refusing to maintain or divorce his first wife.

3. The last instance of formal polygyny occurs when a husband obtains a recalcitrancy order or *nusus* against his wife, and marries another woman. If a woman deserts her husband without just cause and repeatedly refuses to return to him, he may go before a *kathi*, state his position, and ask him to issue a *nusus* decree against her. The *kathi* should issue such an order only after very careful consultation. The order means that until such time as she returns to him and makes obeisance (*ta'at*) the woman is not entitled to be supported by her husband, nor can she claim divorce by *pasah* on the grounds of desertion and non-maintenance. She must therefore earn her own living if her relatives do not support her, and is free to remarry (if she persists in her recalcitrancy) only when her husband dies. He, meanwhile, is of course free to marry again (as many as three other wives simultaneously) and usually does remarry. Cases of *nusus* were very rare in the Colony, however, and there was a strong demand in the Malay Peninsula to restrict its application and to limit the jurisdiction of *kathi* in this matter. One proposal was that only a Chief Kathi with the help of two assessors should be entitled to issue such a decree.

Having disposed of formal polygyny, let us now examine active polygyny, that is, instances of a man cohabiting with more than one wife. First it must be stated that few Singapore Malay women were willing to enter into a polygynous union, and also that not many parents agreed to give their daughters in marriage to a man whom they knew to be already married. When parents did consent to such a union, it was almost always on account of poverty; the man usually bribed them with a large sum of money or they were already indebted to the suitor financially. Sometimes, also, when a young girl was an orphan, her guardians were eager to rid themselves of the responsibility of looking after her and they gave her away to the first suitor, even if they knew him to be already married.

Among Singapore Malays it was generally considered humiliating for a woman to have a co-wife in active polygyny[1] and even more humiliating for both of them to live under the same roof. For that reason, and also in

[1] The wives of a polygynous Malay were sometimes jeered at openly by young children in the neighbourhood.

order to avoid friction in the household, the majority of polygynous men maintained separate establishments if they could afford to do so; or else one wife continued to reside with her parents and was visited at their home. In either case the husband paid for her board, clothes, and other personal expenses. When the two lived apart, the husband sometimes spent alternate nights in each home, or else four or five nights consecutively with each wife in turn. This latter arrangement was particularly favoured if the homes were distant. When both wives lived under the same roof, the husband was usually careful to share his conjugal favours with scrupulous equality in order to avoid complaints, and also made gifts of equivalent value to each of the two women. General opinion was that a man must be wealthy or have a good income in order to be polygynous, and certainly this was so in most of the cases I knew. The four active polygynous unions mentioned, in a suburb of the town, all centred round well-to-do men (two were prosperous businessmen, one managed a very large religious school, and the fourth was a fairly senior civil servant), and in each case the men maintained separate establishments. The only two Malay cases of polygynous unions (these were, of course, co-residential) mentioned in the household schedules of the Social Welfare Department Survey also showed that the husband was in the upper income group of the Malay community, since one was a clerk and the other an accountant.[1]

Usually, when I asked a Malay whether he had more than one wife, the reply was, 'How could I? I hardly earn enough to support one wife.' And if I asked a woman in her husband's presence whether she would mind if he gave her a co-wife, she often said, 'If he can find enough money for me and for another wife, why should I mind?' In point of fact, however, few Malay women accepted with equanimity their husband's remarriage; in such a case they usually asked him to choose between the two and divorce the one or the other. When faced with the ultimatum the husband frequently divorced the older wife; sometimes, however, especially if he had still a strong affection for her, or if her kinsmen brought pressure to bear upon him, or if he had been disappointed in his new marriage, he repudiated the more recent wife. There were also instances when a man, married to a wealthy woman, surreptitiously remarried and visited his bride in the daytime only. If the older wife discovered this and made an angry scene, he agreed to divorce his new wife, rather than lose his wealthy partner. Some Malays also kept their first wife, but regularly married and divorced another woman in addition. I knew of two such cases, and in one of them the husband entered into more than half a dozen short-lived remarriages. In both cases, the husband had married his first wife when he was poor, and he had gradually become prosperous. He believed that this wife had brought him luck, and would therefore on no account divorce her; on the other hand, he often fell in love with younger women and could not resist marrying them.

[1] See above, p. 64.

On the rare occasions when a man of humble means succeeded in retaining two wives—who had to go to work in order to support themselves adequately—he was accused of using some spell on them. It was believed that no woman in her right senses would agree to being a co-wife and earning a living as well, unless she were bewitched into doing so. This suspicion of sorcery also applied to cases of co-wives who were on good terms with each other, or living peacefully together under the same roof. A woman usually expected her co-wife to hate her, to attempt to poison her, or to secure some means of casting a spell upon her or upon their common husband which would cause him suddenly to take her in abhorrence and neglect or divorce her.[1] An older wife would attempt to explain her husband's remarriage by declaring that she was sure the man really did not wish to remarry, but that her co-wife bewitched him into the action; and she went to a magician in order to seek an effective counter-charm to bring the husband back to his senses and make him divorce his new wife.

Among the younger generation of men and women, polygyny was considered reprehensible, especially among those who came into contact with Western ideals of monogamy and of equal rights for men and women. It was these young Malay men and women who made use of the familiar Muslim reinterpretation of the Koranic text regarding polygyny. The text says, in the opening sentences of the Chapter on Women:[2]

'. . . take in marriage of such other women as please you, two or three, or four, and not more. But if ye fear ye shall not act with equity towards so many, marry one only. . . .'

As stated above, this injunction has been interpreted by modern Muslims in most Islamic countries as forbidding polygyny indirectly. I met very few Malays in Singapore who publicly or privately praised polygyny.[3] On the other hand, there were many who condemned the practice in no uncertain terms; the educated among them, on the grounds that it was 'not really' permissible by Islam and in any case degrading to women; and many illiterate villagers on the practical grounds that it led to incessant and unbearable disputes in the household. All the cases of active polygyny I personally came across concerned middle-aged men. One possible line of argument might be that the younger men had not yet achieved sufficient financial security to enable them to enter into polygynous unions. This, however, would not hold true of Singapore Malays because it was precisely the younger Malays, with their enhanced opportunities for education, who

---

[1] cf. H. Granqvist, op. cit., vol 2., pp. 198-9.
[2] Sale G., trans., *The Koran, translated from the Original Arabic*, London, n.d.
[3] This contrasts with the situation observed in Kelantan by Rosemary Firth. In her conclusion to the section on polygyny, she observes that 'the Malay of the villages regards it [polygyny] as a proper and in general desirable practice, to which people conform or not according to their resources, their inclination, and their chances of maintaining a harmonious domestic life'. (op. cit., p. 42.)

generally held more secure and better-paid jobs than men of the older generation.

I did not hear of any cases of friction in the Colony on account of parents who desired their son to take a second wife, when he himself was reluctant to do so. In some Muslim countries, this practice occurs when the first wife is barren. In Singapore, however, such a problem was usually solved either by the young couple adopting a child, or by the husband divorcing his wife and marrying another. I did, however, come across two cases of parents rebuking their sons for contemplating polygynous unions, arguing in each case that their daughter-in-law had been a good and dutiful wife for many years, had borne children, and did not deserve such treatment.

The position in Singapore was not, therefore, that of a serious clash in attitudes to polygyny between the older and younger generations. Rather, the situation was the following: whereas in the old days polygyny used to be condoned, in 1950 educated men and women declared it to be reprehensible and sought justification for this opinion in a reinterpretation of the Koranic text. Moreover, precisely because polygyny occurred on a small scale, modern Malays generally did not regard the problem as a serious one.

5

Children: Birth, Adoption, Socialization

CHILDREN are desired and loved by Malays. They are a source of joy and delight when small and of security to their parents when they grow older. A childless couple is the object of much pity, the woman inevitably sighing with sorrow as she says that she gave birth to no children, and so had to adopt other people's babies. Singapore Malays are aware that blame for a sterile union may be laid at the door of the husband; they point to numerous cases of wives who, after bearing their first husband no children for several years, remarry and prove to be fertile.

It must not be thought, however, that a Malay woman views with pleasure or even equanimity the prospect of childbirth at close and regularly spaced intervals. Fortunately, there is no tradition for the use of instruments in procuring abortions. Many resort to herbal potions,[1] prepared by a local midwife or by other experienced elderly women, which are said to be often effective. Another popular method is drinking the juice of unripe pineapples or a strong ginger potion.

If there is a delay in menstruation of one or two weeks and pregnancy is suspected, many Malay women assert that raw beaten chicken's eggs washed down with a bottle of stout, help to make the woman feel 'very hot' and induce the menstrual flow. A more costly and less frequent alternative is to drink a very large quantity of *brandy tiga bintang* (three-star brandy). Singapore Malay women recognize that these methods are not always effective and sometimes result only in leaving the patient hopelessly drunk and incapable, and still pregnant into the bargain.

Abortion is illegal in the Colony—except, of course, in cases where the continuation of the pregnancy might endanger the mother's health—but there were one or two clinics where Western-trained doctors were said to perform the operation for a substantial fee. Few Malay women, however, went to these clinics either because they had little faith in Western medicine or because they could not afford the payment required.

The use of Western contraceptives was not unknown by Malays, but it was rarely practised. Birth control clinics came into existence in the Colony in 1949 and were later backed by Government: recourse by Malays to these clinics was slight. They said that one fairly successful method for

[1] This is also true of Peninsular Malays. See Rosemary Firth, op. cit., p. 3; and J. D. Gimlette, *Malay Poisons and Charm Cures*, London 1915, pp. 49, 67, 69-70.

both contraception and abortion was the displacement of the uterus by a skilled Malay midwife, who did this by external massage.[1]

CHILDBIRTH

When the labour pains started, the local Malay midwife (either untrained or partly trained in a Government hospital) was sent for. She came with an assistant—usually a woman with no means of support who welcomed an opportunity of earning some money and perhaps eventually learning the profession—and examined the woman's belly. I was present at a confinement in Tanjong and I describe here what I saw.

The patient was a middle-aged woman called Ara. She had already given birth to twelve children (of whom only four sons had survived), and this was her thirteenth confinement. I arrived in the early afternoon shortly after the midwife had been summoned. The labour pains had started two or three hours earlier. In a room adjoining the kitchen Ara sat on the floor on an old mat, very pale and quiet, with the palms of her hands on the floor behind her back. The midwife had very tightly tied a band of cloth about six inches wide around the waist: this was to prevent the child from rising up again in the belly and delaying the time of birth. Three women friends were chewing betel while the midwife sat quietly next to the patient, regularly massaging her back.

At about 6.30 p.m. the baby arrived but for a few minutes not the slightest attention was paid to it, not even to see what the sex was; the midwife was concerned to get the placenta out. When this was finally done, the patient was washed and carried to another part of the room to lie on a mattress. The first drink Ara took was hot water in which turmeric had been dissolved. The midwife paused to explain to me that Malays always give this immediately after confinement—it was cleansing and warming.

She then turned to the baby who had so far been lying on a thin mat, unattended. After tying the umbilical cord she prayed over a pair of scissors and used them to cut the cord. Some lukewarm water and soap had been brought and she gently soaped, rinsed and dried the face and the body. She then took a cup of clear water, put some of it in her mouth and proceeded to run her lips on the baby's face, almost biting it gently with her mouth full of water, on its eyes and nose and mouth, allowing just a little water to escape from her lips.[2] Having done this several times, she gave the baby to her assistant. The latter placed him on her lap, and warmed a sireh leaf on the naked flame of a candle. She gently pressed the warm leaf on every part of the baby's body, often holding the leaf for a few seconds above the candle to keep it warm and testing the heat of the leaf on the palm

[1] A similar practice apparently exists among the Melanau. Cf. H. S. Morris, op. cit., p. 142.

[2] cf. Winstedt, *The Malay Magician*, p. 107: 'A midwife spits on the child she welcomes into the world; this is a gift of a portion of herself, a pledge of union and good-will, a diluted form of blood covenant.'

G

of her hand before applying it again to another part of the baby's body.[1] The baby was then wrapped up in clean clothes, and placed on a large tray close to his mother. This tray had the following items on it: first, there were several pounds of uncooked grains of rice; above the rice were seven sarongs neatly folded and in good condition; and between the sarongs were a few small silver coins. A pillow was placed above that, and the baby's head made to rest on it, while small round pillows like miniature bolsters were placed on either side of the body to prevent the child from rolling over.

After Ara had been given the hot water and turmeric, she was brought a plate of plain boiled rice and ate a few mouthfuls of it. Meanwhile the midwife washed the placenta well, then put it together with several handfuls of salt and tamarind inside a small worn mat which she tied into a bundle and placed at the foot of the mother's mattress. This was to stay there for three days, when it would be buried by the baby's father near the house.[2]

Up to then the atmosphere had been very tense and everybody had looked strained. But now all smiled and laughed and admired the baby, in spite of the great disappointment that it was yet another boy. So far the husband had entered the room for a minute only, when called to help carry his wife from the spot at which she had given birth to the mattress prepared for her at the other end of the room. But now he sat down, smoked, looked at the baby, and the other sons also came. The midwife lit a cigarette, the other women chewed betel, and everybody spoke a little more loudly than usual; there was a definite air of exuberance. I asked what the baby would eat immediately, and Ara's husband showed me a bottle containing about an inch of reddish liquid. He explained it was a type of honey, *gula madu*, very sweet and very expensive, which he had bought at a Chinese shop. They would stir very little of it in some water and give it to the baby for a day or so until his mother would have milk to suckle him.

I visited Ara on the following afternoon. She was sitting up on her mattress and the baby was lying next to her. I was shown that now there. were only six sarongs on his tray; every day one would be removed until on the seventh day there would be none left. The rice would then be cooked as a sweet broth and distributed with the small silver coins to young village children.

In Tanjong as soon as the labour pains started, propitiatory gifts were made to *hantu* (ghosts or spirits) to ensure a prompt and safe delivery. Two dishes were prepared, each consisting of *běrteh* (toasted padi), a hard-boiled hen's egg and three skinned bananas. The contents of each dish

---

[1] In *One Hundred Years of Singapore*, vol. i, p. 511, Dr Gilbert E. Brooke makes some interesting remarks on 'Malay puerperal customs'. He mentions the custom of applying a heated sireh leaf to the body of the new-born baby.

[2] cf. R. J. Wilkinson, *The Peninsular Malays*. 1. *Malay beliefs*, London 1906, p. 30, also p. 52.

were thrown, one in the sea and the other inland in an uninhabited area outside the village. It was not essential for the village magician himself to offer the gifts; any man could do so, but never a woman. A woman, however, could prepare the offerings.

Whenever possible, the offerings were made at night; but if the labour pains started early in the morning and it appeared that the birth was imminent the ritual took place at once. The villagers stressed that the food offered inland was eaten by birds or wild dogs while fish ate the food thrown to the sea; the *hantu* only smelled (*chium*) the offering and, having done so, was satisfied and refrained from harming the mother or the baby. The procedure was referred to as *buang laut, buang darat* (throwing to the sea and inland). Urban Malays in Singapore expressed great surprise when I described the ritual and assured me that it had no counterpart in the town.

POST-NATAL RITES AND CEREMONIAL

About a week after the birth a ceremony called *chuchi lantai* (washing of the floor)[1] was held. The mother and the midwife in turn poured water over each other, the midwife went through the motions of scrubbing the floor and rinsing it with water into which the juice of a lime had been squeezed. If the baby was a boy a hen was offered to the midwife; if a girl, a cock. Large trays of food were also given to the midwife, to her assistant, to any other woman who helped during the birth, and to the village magician if the labour had been long and his services sought.

On the afternoon of the *chuchi lantai* ceremony several male guests were invited to the house to pray and partake of a small meal. I was told that in the urban areas the ceremony was becoming less usual. On the other hand, when it did not take place the midwife received a larger fee to compensate for the lack of food trays and the fowl. However, a week after the birth two or three men were asked to the house to pray and were served coffee or tea with snacks.

One other important ceremony, *mandi tolak bala*,[2] took place soon after the birth of a child, on the forty-fourth day. Up to then the mother had been governed by several taboos which are described below. On the forty-fourth day a man well versed in religious prayers was invited to the house (often several other men were asked to join him); he recited some verses and prayed over a bowl of water into which he squeezed the juice of a lime. The mother later poured the water over her head and body, and this marked the end of the taboo period.

If the household was well-to-do they had then or on the following day

---

[1] W. W. Skeat, *Malay Magic*, London 1900, p. 348, refers to the 'floor-washing ceremony' of Selangor Malays.

[2] *Mandi* means to bathe. *Tolak bala* Wilkinson's dictionary renders as 'a propitiatory offering against misfortune'. The expression is significant; it provides further proof that the woman is believed to go through a dangerous phase, fraught with possibilities of misfortune, during these forty-four days.

another ceremony, that of *potong rambut* (cutting the hair). Large-scale feasting frequently occurred on this occasion. Theoretically, this was the first time the baby's hair was cut, and there was a special ritual. In most cases, however, the *potong rambut* was delayed for months or years until the wedding of a close relative, in order to save expense; meanwhile, of course, the child's hair would have been cut several times without ceremony.

Several taboos governed the period of forty-four days after childbirth.

Food. The mother was allowed very little liquid, and that mainly medicinal bitter herbal potions. She could eat rice in moderate quantities, but no meat or eggs and only certain kinds of fish. She should eat very few vegetables with the exception of a very bitter leaf vegetable called *turi*. Her food did not need to be cooked separately, but it was served separately and she ate it alone. Practically no fruit was permitted.

Appearance. She should wear no jewelry. Her belly was tightly bound with a wide belt several yards long. She wore her hair in a tight bun right on top of her head, and she had to smear her forehead with a special brown paste; these were necessary precautions against eye disease or even blindness, which according to Singapore Malays was a grave danger during the post-natal period.

Sexual Relations were completely forbidden during this period. If a woman had no mother to sleep close to her at night to keep the husband away, a kinswoman was often invited for that express purpose. Islam forbids post-natal intercourse for forty days, but most women appeared unaware of a religious prohibition; they said the ban was only customary, an *adat* ban.

Movement. Mother and child must not leave the house for forty-four days, but the prohibition was much more strict where the baby was concerned.

As a woman felt stronger two or three weeks after confinement, she began to 'cheat', *churi churi*. She ventured just outside the house, placed her bun at a lower angle, and she might put on a pair of earrings. She still counted the days, however, and did not conceal her immense relief on the forty-fifth day and her delight at being now really free to move about, wear jewelry, eat with the household and generally resume a normal existence.

In the case of Javanese immigrants, all taboos were lifted after thirty-five days (seven Javanese weeks), including the ban on sexual relations.[1]

ADOPTION

The institution of adopting children was widespread among Singapore Malays. With few exceptions, it was a conscious means of redistributing

---

[1] H. Subandrio states that in Java prayers and feastings take place on the thirty-fifth day after the child's birth, and she adds: 'If all goes well, the worst part of the childbirth is then over and the mother and child are likely to survive. Sexual intercourse may then be resumed.' Op. cit., pp. 127-8.

children from the homes of those who did not wish to, or could not, keep them to the homes of those who wanted them. The exceptions occurred when a person unwillingly adopted the child of a dead kinsman out of a sense of duty.

In many societies where the mechanism of adoption prevails, it is seen to serve the explicit purpose of ensuring the continuity of a line of descent. Among Singapore Malays, however, there is no lineage system and there are no family surnames. Children were adopted largely because their presence was considered essential in a home. When they were not born, or did not survive, they were adopted to fulfil the emotional need of the childless parents, and to be a source of security in the latter's old age.

There was pride in fertility. If one asked a Malay how many children he had, he usually gave the total number born to him. Only by further questioning did one find that perhaps only one or two had survived, the others having died in childhood. Some parents even counted miscarriages and abortions. An elderly clerk in Government service in Singapore told me he had had twenty-three children from the seven women he had married; ten were boys and eight were girls. 'But that is eighteen in all, what about the other five?' He answered, 'I don't know, they were miscarriages and the sex could not be determined.'

A home without young children was not quite a home. It was common for elderly people, living separately from their married children, to adopt permanently or temporarily one of their grandchildren. Sterility was rarely a direct cause of divorce; usually the couple adopted a child.[1] There were two sources, Malay children and Chinese infant girls. It might seem strange in view of what has just been said, that there were Malays willing to part with their own children. However, this happened only in very special sets of circumstances, as we shall see below.

On the other hand, the Chinese in Malaya, especially those belonging to the lower economic strata, were not always fond of girls, whom they considered a liability ('you spend time and money on feeding and bringing them up, and when they grow up and could be of use you have to marry them off, and they go then to their husband's family; girls are goods on which you lose'). There has been, therefore, a constant source of supply of Chinese baby girls. An adopted Chinese child was called *anak běli*, and an adopted Malay child *anak angkat* (raised child). However, it was more common to refer to both types as *anak angkat*, sometimes using for the bought child the term *anak China angkat* (raised Chinese child). Here, however, *anak angkat* will refer to a Malay child and *anak běli* to a Chinese.

The most striking difference between the adoption of a Chinese baby and that of a Malay was that the Chinese parents sold the child unconditionally and absolutely, expressing no desire to see it again—in fact, often stoutly refusing to do so; whereas Malay parents arranged regularly to visit the child they gave away. Malays preferred boys to girls, but were

[1] cf. Rosemary Firth, op. cit., pp. 25 f.

fond of stating formally that they accepted with gratitude whatever God gave them. Other things being equal, they were more reluctant to part with a son than with a daughter, and consequently there were more female than male *anak angkat*. There were so many varieties of adoption among Singapore Malays, that it is necessary to consider them systematically.

ANAK ANGKAT

1. *Nominal Adoption* occurred for three main reasons:

(*a*) The child was sickly and miserable, and the parents thought this was due to the fact that they were not destined to bring it up in their household. If they were reluctant to give it away, they tried the device of surrendering it only nominally to a woman friend or relative. There is no objection to a male person adopting a child nominally, but this is very rare ('it is only we women who fuss and bother about such things'). A few men are invited to pray and partake of a small meal. The leader of the praying group asks the mother why she has summoned them, and her friend declares formally, 'I pronounce this child to be mine, but I should like this woman to bring it up in her home'; and turning to the real mother, 'Do you agree to do so?' The mother replies, 'Yes, I will help bring up your child, since you say you cannot do it.' In many cases, the child's recovery was said to be instantaneous.

(*b*) Among Malays of Javanese extraction there was a strong belief that if a child and its parent of the same sex were born on the same day of the week, and the child was kept in the same household as this parent, one of the two would die; or at least the child would be always ailing. The best solution was to give it away immediately the cord was cut. In some cases, however, the parents wished to keep the baby and begged a friend or kinswoman to adopt it nominally. It was essential that such a child, after the cord was cut, be taken out of the house and placed a few yards away, preferably near the garbage bin to symbolize throwing away; in fact the child was sometimes given the name *Buang* which means 'thrown away'. The nominal adopter would then pick it up, declaring 'I acknowledge this child as my own', and return it to its parents' house where she would formally request the true mother to help her bring it up in her home.

(*c*) When parents had lost several children of the sex of the one just born, they often arranged for a ceremony of nominal adoption to take place along the lines of either type described above.

In these three cases there rarely was a lasting relationship either between the woman who had nominally adopted the baby and the child, or between the two mothers. There was no system of exchange of gifts or visits, and no duties or corresponding rights.

2. *A System of Fostering* might occur in circumstances such as those cited above, in (*a*), (*b*), and (*c*). There were two additional situations:

(*d*) If either parent was divorced or widowed and had to go out to work, and there was nobody at home who could look after a small child, it was placed in the care of foster parents.

(e) If a person remarried and believed that the new partner would discriminate against the child of a former marriage, the child was sent to a foster-home.

In the first three cases, the real parents usually took back the child to their home when it was about seven or eight years old. Singapore Malays believed that a boy or girl who had survived the first dangerous years of early childhood was fairly safe. In the last two cases (d) and (e) the child often returned to his parental home when he reached his middle teens and was able to look after himself and be of help in the house.

The real parents paid for the maintenance of their child throughout its stay in the home of foster-parents. They provided it with clothing; if the child was in infancy they gave tinned milk; when it was older, rice. In addition, they made small periodical payments (in cash, clothing, or jewelry) to the foster-mother, on their regular visits to her home. It was usual for the foster-mother to live in a different village or suburb of the Colony, but if possible the real parents would select a home not too far away from their own. In case of illness or sudden death, the child's own parents were at once informed.

A foster home was selected with very great care; parents preferred the household to have no other very small children so that enough attention might be given to the newly-arrived child, and the character of the foster-parents was ascertained from their friends and neighbours in the rare cases when they were not related by kinship or directly known. If it was suspected later that the child was not well-treated, or was unhappy, arrangements were made to remove it to another home.

It might be argued that the foster system is not adoption. The reason I include it is that Malays themselves used the word *angkat* in this context and that foster-parents did not look after a child for commercial reasons; it was literally a labour of love. The true parents treated them with respect and there was no haggling about payment. Unless one asked a great many questions, it was not clear whether the *anak angkat* was cared for in return for payment. Moreover, it was not unusual for foster-parents to develop such affection for the child that they begged to have it permanently; the real parents might then agree to surrender it and all payments ceased.

3. *Temporary Adoption.* As a rule, it was only close relatives who took a child in temporary adoption. The reasons might be any of those enumerated above in sections 1 and 2, or there might be other factors:

(a) Parents who were poor and had other children to support accepted the offer of a better-off kinsman to give free board and lodging to the child without prejudice to the rights of the real parents.

(b) The true parents had several other children already, and yielded to requests for a particular child to be temporarily adopted. In this context it must be noted that children between the ages of six and fourteen were used to run errands to nearby shops; adults did not like doing so; they thought it lowering in dignity. Often a grandmother chose the pretext that she had nobody to shop for her to persuade a married son or daughter to give her temporarily one of her grandchildren. A grandmother might adopt for a few years one of her younger granddaughters,[1] or an aunt one of her nieces, to help with cooking and housework. On the other hand, an old woman might openly state that she wanted a grandchild to live with her because she was lonely.

(c) The nearest suitable school might be some distance away from home, and parents asked kinsmen living near the school to take in their child for the duration of his schooling period. On school holidays the child usually returned home.

It will have become clear that temporary adoption took place at varying ages and for varying periods (from one to several years) of the child's life. Regular payments for maintenance were not usually made, perhaps because the arrangement was with close relatives and the child often gave small services in exchange for its board and lodging.

4. *Total, Unconditional Adoption* of Malay children occurred in the following situations:

(a) When the child was illegitimate.

(b) When the parents were extremely poor and had several other young children.

(c) When the mother died soon after childbirth, the father might give away the baby.

(d) When a sibling of either parent or a kinsman, or a very close friend, was childless and the true parents already had several children, they might promise to give away in total adoption the child about to be born, and keep their promise.

(e) When either of the parents who was the guardian of the child was divorced or widowed and considered the child an impediment to earning a living, or to remarriage.

(f) In the case of Javanese, when the child was born on the same day of the week as its parent of the same sex.

(g) When both parents were dead.

Even when adoption was unconditional, it was still the duty of the adoptive parents to inform the true parents of the death of their child immediately after it had occurred, so that they might attend the funeral ceremonies.

It was considered preferable in cases of total adoption, by both sets of

---

[1] In his chapter on Adoption de Moubray says: 'There is quite an everyday reason for adoption not mentioned by Parr and Mackray: *the need of an old woman who has for some reason no daughter in the house to obtain a girl to look after her.*' G. A. de C. de Moubray, *Matriarchy in the Malay Peninsula and Neighbouring Countries*, London 1931, p. 181.

parents, that they live in different villages or districts of the Colony. The reason given was that the real parents would be spared pangs of regret if they did not see the child growing before their eyes.

Another condition of full adoption upon which both sets of parents appeared to be in full agreement was that the child must be transferred at the earliest possible date, usually within a week or two of birth. In such a case, it was said, the real parents would not have had time to form a great attachment to it, and the adopting parents would have the illusion that the baby was truly theirs since they would have had it practically from the day of birth.

If the adoptive parents became very ill or died before the child reached adulthood, and no close relative of the adoptive parents offered him a home, the real parents did so.

Although Malays had no explicit tradition for accepting payment for a child, nevertheless in cases of full adoption it was usual for the adoptive parents to give a sum of money to the true parents, as a consideration. When there had been an agreement before the birth to give the child away, or when the baby was adopted a few days after birth, it was customary for the adopting parents to pay the costs of the delivery; in many cases this might be as large a sum of money as the amount paid to buy a Chinese baby girl. The average payments to a village midwife (the *bidan*) totalled $20, and in addition there was about $15 to $20 to be spent on special medicines (mainly herbal potions for the mother to drink in order to cleanse her body) and on oils for massaging her belly and limbs. Adopting parents did not need to pay all the expenses incurred, but they had to offer at least $20-$30.[1]

Malays said that there was no haggling or bargaining when a Malay child was transferred, and therefore no formal purchase. The parents gratefully accepted whatever amount was freely given, and in later years the financial transaction was alluded to by the adoptive parents only under great provocation. It was also traditional for a couple to give a sum of money to the true parents for a Malay child past infancy who was transferred permanently in unconditional adoption.

Sometimes a Singapore Malay parent who had surrendered his or her child in unconditional adoption regretted the decision. This happened particularly in the case of a widow or divorcée who, some months or years after the transfer of her child, remarried and had a good home. She went to the adoptive parents and in turn pleaded and argued with them; she reminded the child that she was his real mother, and usually succeeded in taking him. The child then had to become readjusted to living with his own mother, and with a stepfather, in a new home and usually in a different district, while the adoptive parents suddenly found themselves back in their childless status.

[1] Rosemary Firth, op. cit., p. 84, mentions one case of a Malay buying for $40 the child of a fellow villager who had lost all his money gambling.

ANAK BĔLI

Adoption of Chinese babies was along much more clear-cut lines than that of Malay *anak angkat*. The babies were almost exclusively of the female sex; indeed not more than a handful of Chinese boys in the Island were known to have been adopted by Malays. This was probably because other Chinese paid for a male child a far higher price than a Singapore Malay could afford.

Normally the transfer was effected through intermediaries. The Chinese parents in question were usually poor; sometimes, however, a prosperous shopkeeper sold one of his baby daughters to a very poor Malay fisherman or unskilled labourer. Again, the younger the baby the happier were the Malays. The price paid for an *anak bĕli*, a girl, varied between $30 and $100. Chinese girls were preferable in two respects to Malay babies: (1) There was no fear or danger that the true parents would claim them back later. (2) The girls were much fairer in complexion than Malays, and the latter are extremely colour-conscious.

There was no acculturation problem for Chinese girls since they were transferred in early infancy. A serious obstacle to their becoming completely identified with Malays, however, was their physical appearance; the two general criteria were their fairer complexion and their marked epicanthic fold. Many Malays have an epicanthic fold, but it is rarely as pronounced as that of the Chinese. Great care was usually taken by adoptive parents to conceal from the child her true identity, but she inevitably guessed it from conversations overheard and above all from her playmates who soon discovered this exceptionally successful way of teasing or hurting her.

Among wealthier Malays an *anak bĕli* was sometimes given a large share of domestic chores if the couple already had other children of their own. This practice, however, was very rare and was frowned upon by Singapore Malays. They prided themselves quite justifiably on being fairer in their treatment of *anak bĕli* than the Chinese or Arab sections of the population were. These two other groups had a long tradition of buying Chinese infant girls who were destined to become unpaid domestic servants as soon as they were old enough to be useful, from the age of seven or eight years onwards.

The tradition of adopting children appears to be long established among Malays. Certainly no living Malay could remember the time when the institution was a novelty. In my 1949 survey of Tanjong (which had then 48 Malay households), I found 18 adopted children in 16 households. A child for the purpose of the survey was a person under fifteen years of age. There were a total of 92 children. There were 12 fully adopted *anak angkat* (8 girls and 4 boys) in 12 households. Two infants, a boy and a girl, were each being cared for by foster-parents in two different households. Finally there were 4 *anak bĕli* (all girls) in 3 households. Of the 12 *anak angkat* most were doubly orphaned and very closely related to one of the adoptive parents, being usually the child of a sibling of the latter. The 4 *anak běli* had all been bought when only a few days old. Two households had each one *anak běli*, while one household had two. In addition to the 18 children, there were 3 young unmarried adopted girls over the age of fifteen. One of them was an *anak angkat* living from childhood in the home of her father's sister, who was childless. Another was also an *anak angkat*, adopted by her dead mother's sister. The third girl was an *anak běli*.

As can be seen from these figures, the number of transferred children was by no means negligible. In this particular area there were adopted children in one third of the total number of households (16 out of 48). About one in five of the children in the village (18 out of 92) lived in an adoptive home. These figures do not, of course, take into account the children born to members of the community and given away to homes outside Tanjong.[1]

A child who was taken in full and unconditional adoption grew up as an 'own' child and had, on the whole, the same marriage prospects as that of the true children of the adoptive parents.

A Malay child taken from infancy in full adoption used his or her adoptive father's name for most purposes; but at a religious ceremony (such as a burial) and on official documents the true father's name was mentioned lest the sacrament or procedure be void. However, in the case of an illegitimate child, when arrangements were made for its adoption before its birth, the adoptive father might make a false declaration, registering the baby as his own in the birth certificate. There was one such case in Tanjong.

At school and on informal occasions an *anak běli* generally used her adoptive father's name. On the other hand, at all religious ceremonies and even on official documents (such as marriage and divorce registers) she was stated to be *binti* Abdullah. The tradition in Singapore was for all non-Muslims who became converted to Islam in order to join the Malay community (*masok Mělayu*) to change both their personal name and their patronymic. An *anak běli* or a person who *masok Mělayu* might be given any personal name,[2] but it was always followed by *bin* or *binti* Abdullah. Abdullah is also a name used by Malays, and in Arabic it means worshipper of God.

Finally, it should be mentioned that although among Singapore Malays the institution of adoption of children was widespread and of long standing, until the end of 1950 when the Children and Young Persons Ordinance

---

[1] Rosemary Firth, op. cit., p. 4, in a survey of a rural area on the North-East Coast of Malaya, found that 53 out of a total of 465 children (about one in nine) were being cared for by others than their parents.

[2] It was usual, however, for a Chinese woman who *masok Mělayu*, and often for a Chinese adopted girl, to be called Aminah. The name is of the same root as the Arabic word for 'believer'.

came into force, there was no legal obligation to register the transfer of a child.[1] There had been, however, provision for the legal adoption of children since 1939. Recourse by Malays to this procedure, which was costly and somewhat complex, was negligible.[2] The new Ordinance made the registration of transferred children compulsory. The term 'transferred child', however, had a limited meaning. It applied to a female under the age of fourteen living apart from her natural father or mother, but it did not include a girl living with a grandparent, a sibling, or a brother or sister of a deceased parent by the whole blood. This legislation thus would not affect Malays (or others) who adopted boys; but it affected those who adopted girls, with the exceptions just quoted and with some other minor exceptions.

SOCIALIZATION OF THE CHILD

Infancy and Early Childhood

A Malay child starts life with one great asset: he is almost never unwanted. True, Malay women resort to abortifacients, but once a child is born it is dearly loved. Its parents and siblings rejoice to see it, be it male or female, and the usual duties of feeding it, changing its clothes, and nursing it when it is teething or has the stomach-ache, appear to weigh very lightly upon its mother. If it is a first or second child, there is the cheerful assistance of her own mother and sisters; and if she has other growing children they, in turn, find joy in tending the new baby.

Whether a Malay child was really hungry, or simply wanted the maternal breast for comfort, it was there for him to have at his leisure and pleasure, not only in the first few months when he had no other food, but also later when he could walk and talk and partake of adult nourishment. The baby's existence, however, was not centered around his mother's physical presence. He spent several hours a day being carried in the arms, or across the hip, of other members of the household, of young neighbours, of visiting relatives and friends. At this stage physical caresses were lavish and the small baby was looked after with indulgence, attentive care, and cheerful patience.

When the child was about eight or nine months old he was left free to crawl about the floor of the house, while his siblings or parents looked on. He often went dangerously near the open fire in the kitchen and cooking implements such as choppers, knives, and coconut graters. His mother did not spend time or effort ordering him out of the kitchen, or snatching away a sharp knife. On the contrary, she let him come as near to the fire as he

[1] There was one exception. In 1933 it became illegal to acquire young girls for domestic service. This institution, known as the *Mui Tsai* system, was a recognized practice in South China and among Chinese in the Colony. The 1933 Ordinance also required all existing *mui tsai* to be registered. Malays were not affected by this legislation, as they did not have *mui tsai*.

[2] For the years 1940 to 1949 inclusive, records show only 3 Malay adopting parents. Two of the three children adopted were Malays.

could with comfort and calmly remark, 'hot, eh?' until the heat drove him away; or she let him handle a sharp knife and even cut himself, and observe, 'sharp, eh?', washing the blood away and drying his tears while she carried on with her cooking. This attitude, at first startling to a Western observer, seemed a sensible manner of dealing with a toddler's natural curiosity and desire to handle everything. Accidents in the home were rare, and very small children learned to avoid injury when walking barefoot on a dirty track full of sharp stones, fallen branches of trees, discarded tins and broken bottles. Singapore Malay children learned essentially by example and by trial and error, not by admonition or corporal punishment.

Supreme importance was attached to emotional well-being and a host of physiological ailments ranging from diarrhoea to fever were frequently attributed to the fact that the child was *rindu*, or pining, for someone who was away. Parents and grown-up siblings went to great lengths to satisfy a child's yearning for their presence; a man might be urgently called away from the wedding of a close kinsman in another district and asked to return home at once because his child was fretting for him.

Weaning usually occurred when a child was in its third year. However, a child might be weaned much earlier if a younger sibling was born, as the strain of suckling two babies simultaneously was said to be too great for the mother. I observed no differentiation in the ages of weaning boys and girls, and there was none in theory. When I put the question directly to parents they expressed great surprise that anybody should think there might be discrimination in favour of either sex.

Malays were fully aware of the deprivation which weaning entailed for a child and they preferred on the whole that the initiative come from it, and not from the mother, that it should just 'not want' the breast any more of its own accord.

Bed-wetting frequently continued until a child was two or three years old, and sometimes even four or five, but no punishment was inflicted.[1] One must remember, of course, that the majority of Singapore Malays slept on mats on the floor, that a mat is easily washed and dried, and that bed-wetting did not produce on the Malay mother the harassing effect it does on a Western mother. Sphincter control also was not considered a matter of particular importance, and the frequent practice of leaving small babies between the ages of three or four months and a year naked from the waist downwards reduced the amount of dirty clothing. The mess made on the floor-boards was quickly washed, as was the child. If by accident a child soiled an adult's clothes, or a mattress, he was not scolded if he was as yet too small to be able to walk or talk.

Here it must be explained that Singapore Malays, especially those in the

---

[1] I found the same situation in areas of Java and Sumatra in 1954. Moreover, a European Nursing Adviser who lectured to nurses in Java told me that when she discussed bed-wetting as a problem and as a symptom of psychological disturbance, her students looked at her in amazement.

rural areas, referred to the various stages of a child's life not by his age in years, but by other symbols. These were mainly *pandai jalan* (lit. clever at, or capable of, walking); *pandai chakap* (clever at talking); *pandai lari* (lit. clever at running); *sěkolah* (lit. school, i.e. going to school); and for a boy *pandai chari makan* (clever at searching for food, i.e. earning a living). This last term usually applied to adolescent boys who had started work. The age of puberty for girls was clearly described as such, with the additional specification for a girl who was expected to have her first menses in the very near future of *mahu anak dara* (about to become a maiden). A girl who wanted to refer to the period when she was about eleven or twelve years old used the expression *bělum datang kotor* (not yet come dirty, i.e. not yet menstruated) or *bělum datang bulan* (not yet come the month).

Birthdays were not celebrated, and dates generally were not remembered (with the exception of deaths, which necessitate special memorial prayers at regular intervals). However, sophisticated parents, such as clerks or schoolteachers, usually knew the ages of their children accurately, and urban parents (unlike those in the countryside) as a rule had fairly precise notions of age.

Differentiation Between Kin and non-Kin

How did a small child come to differentiate between kin and non-kin, and at what age did such a process occur? The matter is of interest from the standpoint of the individual development of a child's attitudes to the persons he meets. It is also of theoretical importance to the anthropologist to assess the significance which a society attaches to the need for a child's differentiating between kin and non-kin. In Upper Egypt, for instance, Ammar tells us that parents teach their children kinship terms from early childhood and that by the age of five a child is able to distinguish various categories of kin, and to use the correct terms for father's sibling, mother's sibling, parent's sibling's child, and own sibling's child.[1] He adds[2]: 'The recognition of blood relation . . . is usually used as a test for young children by their elders: one might hear an elder questioning a younger, "Who is your uncle? Who is your cousin? Where do they live? Whom do you prefer?" and so on.'

Among Singapore Malays the position was strikingly different. There was no deliberate effort by parents to teach their young children to differentiate between *saudara* (kinsmen) and *orang lain* (strangers), or to learn to apply the kinship terms correctly. Young children who were six or seven (and frequently well above that age) had only the haziest knowledge of their kinship relations to others than their own parents, siblings, and grandparents. Neither did they always know whether to use the term *saudara* when referring to a person with whom they were very familiar and who might well be a neighbour or frequent visitor to their household, but

[1] Hamed Ammar, *Growing Up in an Egyptian Village*, London 1954, p. 131.
[2] op. cit., p. 132.

no kinsman. In Singapore Malay society a consanguineous or affinal link did not always go hand in hand with familiarity and ease between the persons concerned; this was often due to geographical inaccessibility. A small child might be much more familiar and friendly with a neighbour than with a parent's sibling who lived some miles away. Moreover, he would be taught to address an elderly neighbour by the term reserved for grandparents, *datok* or *nenek*.[1] In such a context, it is not surprising that young children found it difficult to discern kin from non-kin since neither the system of nomenclature nor the immediately apparent behavioural attitudes always served as reliable guides.

However, as a child reached the early teens he usually came to distinguish true *saudara* from those whom he addressed by merely 'courtesy' kinship terms.

Indulgence and Discipline

Singapore Malay fathers are far from being disciplinarians and often show more indulgence than their wives towards the children. If a child misbehaves, it is more often the mother than the father who punishes him.[2] Indeed, many conjugal arguments occur when the father comes home in the evening and discovers that one of the children has been beaten during the day; he may rebuke his wife seriously, in the presence of the child, for being cruel or impatient. One often finds in Malay society the reverse of the common threat in Western society, of 'Wait till father comes home and I tell him what you have done!'; in the Malay situation it is quite frequently, 'You are misbehaving because father is at home and spoils you, eh?'. Fathers also show even less resistance than mothers to their children's requests for pocket-money. In spite of this, children when they grow up still go to their mother when in trouble, and if they want to acquaint their father with the news that they have lost their job, or are unhappy in their married life, or are short of money, they usually do so through their mother.

Malays expressed indulgence towards their small children chiefly in the giving of pocket-money or *bĕlanja*. However, while young toddlers were allowed lavish sums, growing children of six or seven years found their allowance gradually decreased until in their early teens it was only a small fraction of the amount they had in early childhood. At the age of three, a child was given daily amounts varying from 10 or 20 cents to 50 or 60 cents, and in some cases the upper limit represented about a quarter or a third of the total daily income of the household. The pocket-money, however, might be spent on 'food' snacks such as cakes, savouries, or bananas; but

[1] Of course, there is here an exact parallel with the practice of some English parents who teach small children to address, and refer to, a woman friend of the family as 'auntie'.

[2] cf. the situation among the Land Dayaks: 'Only very occasionally are children chastised, but then it is usually by the mother.' W. R. Geddes, *The Land Dayaks of Sarawak*, H.M.S.O., London 1954, p. 35.

sometimes the whole amount went to buy water-ices, chewing gum, or a bottle of sweetened coloured water. Most parents appeared unable to resist the constant demands for 5 cents and 10 cents, and explicitly declared that small children were entitled to *bĕlanja*.[1] I could observe no differentiation whatever in the sums given to boys and to girls.

A question which we may well ask is this. What effect did the tradition of giving large sums of pocket-money to children have (a) on general household discipline, and (b) on the commercial discipline of Singapore Malays? As far as the former is concerned, it is important to remember that indulgence in this respect was restricted to very small children; a schoolchild was firmly told that he was no longer a baby and did not require humouring or pampering. Behaviour towards toddlers and towards children who were upwards of about six years of age was very clearly differentiated, and the spending of large sums of pocket-money was looked upon as one of the concomitants of early childhood. Older siblings usually accepted the position, were flattered by the implication that they were now more responsible and reasonable, and friction in the household on account of jealousy of a younger child's *bĕlanja* was rarely serious. As for general commercial discipline, it would be rash to assume that great indulgence in giving pocket-money to small children is directly or indirectly responsible for the lack of interest in saving or in accumulating capital which characterized the majority of Singapore Malays. A growing child became aware at an early age that his parents did not have unlimited funds; that they often delayed buying essential items of food or clothing until his father's wages were paid; that frequently his mother pawned or sold her gold ring, bracelets, or valuable sarong, in order to obtain money; and that it was only very small children unaware of the realities of life who would ask for 5 or 10 cents several times a day.[2] Before a Malay reached adolescence and was able to earn his own living, he had fully realized for many years the value of money in his society.

An obedient and well-behaved child was openly praised both by his own kinsmen and by neighbours and friends. A little girl of seven or eight who was quiet, tidy in her appearance, willing to fetch and carry for adults and to look after babies of kinsmen or neighbours, earned the esteem of all concerned and was labelled *budak baik*, a good child. A young boy who cheerfully ran errands, spoke politely to his elders, was content with a small daily sum of pocket-money, and was generally good-tempered, was also *budak baik*. Adults said that children were very sensitive to praise, and that appreciation acted as a further incentive to continued good behaviour.

[1] I found the same situation in two urban areas in Java in 1954.
[2] cf. Rosemary Firth, op. cit., p. 88. She reports a comment by a villager about the extravagance of some children in spending money on sweetmeats: 'Yes, they are spoilt . . . but then they are young. When they grow older, they will understand and not be always asking for cents for sweets.'

Children were secure in the knowledge that their parents would always protect them, and look after them and comfort them in their sorrows. However, it was not customary for them to report every small incident, or ask their father or mother to avenge them for some injury suffered at the hands of a playmate. If a boy was extremely quarrelsome or aggressive, other boys jeered at him or blankly refused to play with him, but they did not as a rule ask adults to arbitrate. Boys and girls learned at a tender age, even before they were five or six, to observe silently and to abstain from comment, and not to tell tales or repeat gossip. A first principle of behaviour which a child was taught both by example and by explicit injunction was that he must not divulge any details about the happenings in his household, or his group of kin, however harmless he may believe the information to be. He learned to be evasive or absent-minded when faced with a direct question from an outsider, and if need be he cheerfully lied either by giving an answer contrary to the truth or by claiming complete ignorance of the subject. He learned that generally the less one said, the smaller the likelihood of being rebuked later for lack of discretion.

In some societies, young children who have misbehaved can run away from home to the house of a kinsman in order to avoid their father's or mother's wrath; and the existence of a large circle of indulgent kinsmen might be said to dissipate the aggression and friction which inevitably arise between parents and children living in a small household. This mechanism, however, did not generally operate among Singapore Malays. Apart from the fact that severe corporal punishment was infrequent, and that parental anger was rarely so frightening to a young child as to cause him to run away from home, young children did not usually visit their kinsmen's houses freely. They went there when sent on an errand, or in the company of their own parents. Moreover, the paternal or maternal right to punish an erring child was not questioned or interfered with, except by the child's grandparents if they believed the punishment to be cruelly administered. However, it was unusual for a child to run to the near-by home of a grandparent for protection or to tell spontaneously of a beating. Children who were punished did not whine or complain, they stayed at home until they had regained their composure, and when they went out they exhibited no obvious signs of grief or of tears.

Apart from physical blows, one form of punishment for serious misdemeanours—such as theft of money—was withholding food altogether for one meal.

When the child went to school, he found himself for the first time among strangers in a strange physical environment and under the discipline of strangers. This was usually so in urban and suburban areas, although not in village schools. In the latter, the building itself was in the village, the schoolteachers were intimately known, most of the pupils had been playmates and neighbours, and the experience was rarely strange or frightening. Although there was stricter discipline at school than at home, corporal

H

punishment was officially discouraged in Government schools. Singapore Malay parents stated that only those who fed and sheltered a child had the right to chastise it, but they allowed religious teachers more authority than lay teachers in this context.

From the age of about six years onwards, children ran errands to local shops and to neighbouring houses. Some young children of school age were also used to hawk snacks during their out-of-school hours and walked cheerfully along lanes and streets chanting their wares—cakes, savouries, fried bananas. Often, a woman who had no child or grandchild would pay the son of a neighbour or of a friend a few cents to hawk her snacks for her, and this money belonged to the boy to do with as he pleased. She might also employ a young girl. In some districts services were highly organized on a percentage basis, and the youngsters were given on the average ten per cent commission on the sale price; they thus acquired at an early age some insight into the value of their labour. This, however, was work which was considered unsuitable after the age of about twelve years.

Girls were more useful than boys about the house. If there was no piped water they fetched bucketfuls from the well. They helped with the daily grinding of spices and with cooking generally, they looked after the younger children in the household, they cleaned the rooms. In the rural areas, if the economy centred around rubber-tapping many children helped their parents with the actual job of collecting the rubber; and in a fishing village the boys sometimes went fishing for prawns after school hours or during school holidays, and helped in the care and maintenance of boats and fishing tackle, while some of the girls learned from their mothers how to make and repair nets.

Circumcision

Strictly speaking, the word *sunat* (Arabic *sunnah*) means the following of the Prophet's example, a commendable but not obligatory practice. Singapore Malays, however, use the word to denote specifically circumcision for boys and clitoridectomy for girls. Contrary to popular belief among both Muslims and non-Muslims, circumcision is not given paramount importance in Muslim canon law. It is certainly not one of the five pillars of Islam. Yet throughout the Muslim world circumcision is universally practised, while some of the pillars, such as daily prayers and fasting during the whole month of Ramadan, are often neglected.

Among Singapore Malays circumcision usually took place between the ages of twelve and fifteen years. It did not represent a crucial stage in a man's life: a circumcised boy did not get admitted into adolescent or adult groups by mere virtue of the fact that he had undergone the operation.[1]

---

[1] The age of majority according to all schools of Islam is normally puberty. 'Puberty is conclusively presumed at the end of the fifteenth year and may occur as early as the twelfth year in a boy or the ninth year in a girl.' S. Vesey-Fitzgerald, op. cit., p. 103.

Circumcised and uncircumcised boys played and worked together, and could alike enter a mosque and pray in it. There were instances of boys being circumcised when they were only ten or eleven years old, as when a younger brother was operated on at the same time as his older brother to save the cost of a separate feast later. Malays stressed that the younger a boy was circumcised the better, because the wound healed more quickly; they added, however, that the ceremony was usually postponed until the age of fourteen or fifteen because of lack of funds. Parents liked to throw as lavish a feast as possible and delayed the event in the hope of acquiring more capital. Sometimes two brothers pooled their resources and had their sons circumcised on the same day. The cost of a circumcision feast varied from $30 to $100 according to the scale of the feasting.

I said in an earlier chapter that boys were taught to read and recite the Koran by a religious teacher. When they were considered by the latter to have acquired sufficient mastery of the subject—this usually meant that they could fluently read aloud the Holy Book from cover to cover, without necessarily understanding the meaning—their parents celebrated the event with a ceremony known as *khatam Koran* (finishing the Koran). The boy, dressed in new clothes and adorned, took his seat on a dais and read a portion of the Book, in the midst of a large congregation of guests. Then he made obeisance to his religious teacher, to whom were presented several yards of white cloth, a *songkok* (cap), a pair of slippers, an umbrella, and a kettle. This last item was for use when making ablutions before prayer.

Not all parents went to the expense of having a special *khatam Koran* ceremony. Many contented themselves, when their sons had completed their course, with sending the religious teacher a tray of cooked glutinous rice and hard boiled eggs, ornamented with paper flowers. Some people, on the other hand, combined a *khatam Koran* feast with circumcision; on such occasions the *khatam Koran* took place on the evening preceding the day of circumcision.

The operation was made preferably very early in the morning, when it was still cool, and the boy was bathed in cold water: 'When he is cold, he does not feel the pain so much.' The man who operated was known as the *tukang sunat* and he used very simple tools, severing the foreskin with a razor, and bandaging the wound with a home-made ointment. The patient was held on the lap of an older friend of his father and as a rule submitted stoically to the ordeal. Unless the wound became infected, it was said to heal within a week. The feasting, and most of the praying, took place on the previous evening, only male guests being invited.[1]

Whereas circumcision for boys involved elaborate feasting, clitoridectomy for girls was a very ordinary affair. The operation itself, of course, was much simpler and less painful. I was able to witness it in Tanjong. It

---

[1] My husband attended a circumcision ceremony performed on two young boys in a Malay village, and the feast and praying on the evening preceding the ceremony. I am indebted to him for a description of what he saw on these occasions.

was usually performed by the village midwife and consisted in paring off an extremely small piece of the clitoris. It was done among local Malays between the ages of four and six years with a minimum amount of ceremony; there was very little bleeding and within a few minutes the girl stopped crying and appeared to have forgotten the incident, joining in play with her comrades. No great thought was given to the time and place of the operation. Often, a girl was *sunat* on the day her mother or some other kinswoman had a *chuchi lantai* ceremony; this was probably because the midwife was present on such an occasion and trays of food had already been prepared. After the operation the midwife was given one or two dollars and a small tray of food.

Among immigrant Javanese it was common to perform clitoridectomy on the girl on the thirty-fifth day after her birth, the day all post-natal taboos are lifted. It was also the midwife who officiated. On that day, of course, there was always some praying to mark the end of the seven Javanese weeks after childbirth, and a special meal was prepared to offer the men invited to pray. A tray of food was presented separately to the midwife, and she was given a small fee. As far as circumcision was concerned, the immigrant population followed the same general lines as the local Malays, except that among the former feasting tended to be on a more elaborate scale. Further, the immigrants liked to combine a circumcision feast with a *khatam Koran* celebration, whenever practicable. The age at which the operation took place was the same for boys of both groups.

The fact that circumcision and *khatam Koran* ceremonies were often combined did not mean that circumcision was a mark of religious competence. In the first place, not all Malay boys were made to persevere in their studies until they attained the proficiency necessary to *khatam Koran*, but all Malay boys were circumcised irrespectively of the state of their religious erudition. In the second place, a circumcised boy who had not yet completed his course of Koran-reading continued his visits to the teacher's house in the company of his fellow-pupils and enjoyed no change of status among them. Every Malay boy was circumcised but every Malay boy did not *khatam Koran*. Also a Malay boy who had *khatam Koran* did not become admitted on this account to adolescent or adult society, but continued to have the same playmates as before. Indeed, the combination of the two ceremonies, when it did occur, was simply a means of saving expense. I once saw a young man go through a *khatam Koran* ceremony a few hours before he was due to sit in state with his bride, again to save expense; he had been circumcised before he had completed his religious tuition. As a rule, however, it was more common for brides than for grooms to combine a *khatam Koran* ceremonial with their wedding.

The whole process of socialization of the child was based on a deliberate attempt by parents to make their offspring grow into peaceful and well-behaved human beings. The primary aim of Singapore Malay parents—

with few exceptions—was not to have 'successful' children in the sense of wealthy and socially prominent adults, but to have children who derive happiness from personal relationships. They hoped that their sons would be contented in their job and happy in their home life, and that their daughters would become good housekeepers and loving mothers.

6

Divorce

FOR several decades up to 1950, divorce had been so frequent that annually, for every hundred Malay marriages taking place in Singapore, there had been about fifty divorces. What are the implications of this in theoretical terms? Do Malays regard marriage as a permanent relationship, or as a partnership easily terminated? How do attitudes towards the conjugal bond accord with other characteristics of Malay personal relationships? Are economic adjustments at divorce easily made, or otherwise? What are the effects of the dissolution of a union upon the young children of the couple, and upon the kinsmen of the couple?

After looking at some of the aspects of divorce, we should be in a position to answer at least some of these questions. We must consider therefore: (1) legal aspects, (2) divorce procedure, (3) causes of divorce, (4) economic aspects, (5) custody of children, (6) repercussions of divorce.

LEGAL ASPECTS

For a Muslim couple to be divorced, the husband must pronounce a ritual formula, stating to his wife, 'I divorce you'. If he says it only once or twice in succession, that is to say, pronounces one or two *talak*, the woman is divorced automatically but may not remarry for one hundred days. During that period (known as *iddah*) the couple live apart and the husband may, if he wills, revoke the divorce and take his wife back in marriage. This revocation is known as *rojo* (an Arabic word meaning 'return'). If the divorce has not been revoked, after the hundred days have elapsed and provided she is not pregnant, the wife is free to marry any other man. Theoretically the *iddah* should cover three menstrual periods to ascertain whether the woman is pregnant, but in Singapore the fixing of a term of one hundred days has been thought adequate for the purpose. If the wife is pregnant her husband can still persevere with the divorce, but in Muslim law he is bound to maintain her until she is confined and for the length of time after her confinement that she suckles the new-born infant.

If the husband pronounces a triple *talak*, stating 'I divorce you three times', or saying three times in succession, 'I divorce you', the divorce is irrevocable. If the couple wish to marry again the wife must first be married to, and divorced by, another man. This provision acts as a very efficient check on a hasty triple *talak*, as the intermediate marriage, according to Muslim law, must be also consummated.

A Muslim need not give any reasons for divorcing his wife, the divorce is not granted by the *kathi*, but merely *registered* by him after it has been pronounced by the husband. There are only a few instances where Shafi'i law allows a *kathi* to pronounce a judicial decree of divorce known as *pasah* (Arabic *faskh*): in the case of desertion and lack of maintenance by the husband over a number of years, or where the husband is impotent, or abjures Islam.

When the marriage contract is prepared it is possible for the bride's guardian to insist upon the attachment of special conditions known as *ta'alik*. A *ta'alik* may state, for instance, that should the husband prevent his wife from meeting her parents freely, or should he request her to follow him to any other country, he now undertakes that such behaviour on his part will entitle his wife to become automatically divorced by him. In other words, on the day the marriage contract is signed, he pronounces this conditional divorce to become effective later at her request.

So far, then, the following forms of divorce have been mentioned: *talak*, *pasah*, and *ta'alik*. In addition, there is divorce by purchase or redemption, *khula*, known in Malay as *tĕbus talak* (*tĕbus* means redeem).[1]

Divorce by *khula* occurs when the wife seeks a divorce from a reluctant husband. She may then offer him a sum of money, or some form of property, in compensation. There is a Tradition of the Prophet on the subject. Sabith's wife wanted to be repudiated by him, but he was unwilling. She went to seek the Prophet's advice and he asked her whether she was agreeable to surrendering the garden which her husband had given her as 'dowry', in order to persuade him to pronounce the *talak*. She replied eagerly that she would willingly give him the garden, and more. But the Prophet is said to have replied, 'Nay, not more'.[2]

On the other hand, Nawawi in his authoritative manual of Shafi'i law, *Minhaj et Talibin*, says (in the translation *khula* is rendered as 'divorce' while other forms are given as 'repudiation'): 'Divorce is the separation of husband and wife for a compensation paid by the wife, whether the husband uses the word "repudiation" or the word "divorce" . . . Compensation has neither a maximum nor a minimum.'[3]

In 1949 and 1950, appeals against a *kathi*'s decision in this or in other matters within his jurisdiction lay to the Registrar of Mohammedan Marriages. In turn the Registrar's decisions or orders were open to revision by the Governor of the Colony.

Custody of the children of a divorced Muslim couple in the Colony followed English law. In case of dispute, and if the *kathi* was unable to settle the issue amicably (since a *kathi*'s authority in this field was only of

[1] E. N. Taylor in 'Mohammedan Divorce by Khula', *Journal of the Royal Asiatic Society, Malayan Branch*, vol. xxi, Part II, 1948, discusses the law of the Colony with regard to divorce generally, and cites in detail two cases of disputes concerning *khula*, one in Penang and the other in Singapore.   [2] E. N. Taylor, op. cit., p. 27.

[3] Nawawi, *Minhaj et Talibin*, translated by E. C. Howard from the French edition of L. W. C. Van Den Berg, London 1914, p. 320.

an advisory nature), the parents appeared before one of the Civil Courts of the Colony. The judges then made the ruling which they believed to be in the best interests of the children.

The Shafi'i school of Islam states that the mother has the prior right to custody of the children until the age of seven years. The general principle, however, is that the mother must be a Muslim, of sound mind, of good moral behaviour, and resident in an abode which can have no harmful effects upon the children. Moreover, the mother loses her right to the custody of her children if she remarries with a man not related to the children within the prohibited degrees of marriage, or if she is cruel to the children. As the number of eligible men who are related to her children within the prohibited degrees is very small, this means in effect that on remarriage the mother usually loses her right to the custody of her children. There is no analogous limitation to the father's remarriage with respect to his right to the custody of his children by a former union.[1] On the whole, therefore, after early childhood the mother has only a limited right in the Shafi'i school of Islam to the custody of her children. In the Colony, however, the law in relation to custody of the children was English law.

DIVORCE PROCEDURE

Theoretically, it is sufficient for a Muslim to declare to his wife that she is divorced for the fact to become automatically established. For practical purposes, however, it is necessary to register divorces, and in Singapore there were thirteen *kathi* (12 *kathi* and one Chief *kathi*) in various districts who were competent to effect such registration.

A Malay may in a moment of anger say to his wife that she is divorced, and according to Islam she should from that moment live apart from him. But if he does not go at once to the *kathi* to register the fact, the couple sometimes make up the quarrel and forget that the fateful words were mentioned, especially if there were no witnesses. This is not a frequent occurrence, for generally husbands are careful not to use the words lightly. Should a man have decided upon the matter, he usually informs his wife and goes to the *kathi* in his district to register the divorce, stating the number of *talak*. He then gives his wife a copy of this registered declaration (a *surat chĕrai* or letter of divorce), and thereupon the two part. The overwhelming majority of Malay divorces are of the *talak satu* (one *talak*) variety. This means that the husband has the option of revoking the divorce within one hundred days of having pronounced it. He also has this privilege if he has pronounced a two *talak* divorce formula. Three *talak* constitute an irrevocable divorce and a Malay rarely pronounces this; for then the boats are burnt, and should he change his mind and want to take his wife back, there will be the unpleasantness of seeing the woman first married

---

[1] See Sayed Ameer Ali, *Mahommedan Law*, Vol. ii, Calcutta 1929, pp. 251 ff. Also R. Levy, *An Introduction to the Sociology of Islam*, 2 vols, Vol. 1, London 1931, p. 200.

to another man. It is usually an expensive affair, moreover, for the costs of the intermediate marriage and divorce fall upon the husband who wants his wife back. A triple *talak* is not popular also because of a strong belief that a husband who has thus repudiated his wife will constantly feel troubled in his own mind, as if demented, either because he will want his wife back and realize the grave obstacles in the way; or else because there is something inherent in the very act of a triple *talak* which automatically causes serious emotional disorders in the man concerned. This is called *gila talak, talak* madness.

Let us assume that a man has pronounced the *talak satu* and given his wife her *surat chĕrai*. The pair part company at once. A few weeks later the husband may change his mind, or close relatives act as mediators, or sometimes his wife asks to be taken back. He can then at little cost (the fee is $1) go to the *kathi* and register a revocation of his divorce. Such a revocation can take place within the hundred days of the *iddah* period. After that, there must be a proper remarriage as the woman has become a free agent and a potential wife for any Muslim. However, if pregnancy has become manifest during the intervening hundred days, she may remarry only her own husband, the father of the child she is bearing; remarriage with another man is possible only after the birth of the child.

Whether the first *talak* has been revoked, or whether a remarriage in order has occurred between the same parties after the *iddah* period, the fact that this *talak* was pronounced is not obliterated. For should the couple again become divorced by the husband repudiating his wife with one *talak*, the effect is cumulative: two *talak* are now recorded as having been pronounced by the husband. He still, however, can revoke this second *talak* within the hundred days immediately following its declaration, or again allow the period to lapse and take his wife in formal marriage a third time. But now he must be cautious; for should he again pronounce one *talak*, it means in fact three and an irrevocable divorce, since the last *talak* is added to the first two. After that, should the couple want to come together again, they can do so only after an intermediate marriage and a divorce have been arranged. In Muslim law this intermediate marriage must be fully consummated. In practice, however, it is common for the husband to seek a poor and elderly man who for a consideration will undertake to act the part of groom for a day without cohabiting with the temporary wife whom he agrees to divorce the next day. Nevertheless, the woman will have again to observe the *iddah* period of one hundred days before she can remarry her original husband. The intermediate husband is known in Arabic as *muhallil*. Singapore Malays popularly call him *China buta* or 'blind Chinaman'. The origin of the phrase is not known; it is unlikely that the reference is to an actual Chinese man as a Malay woman could only marry a Muslim, and Muslim Chinese are extremely few in number in the country.[1] Only destitute men with very

[1] Mr J. M. Gullick has drawn my attention to the fact that Wilkinson in his

little dignity consent to play the *muhallil*, a role which is considered degrading. The procedure of going through an intermediate wedding in order to resume the original marriage relationship is extremely rare. I heard only of two actual cases during my stay in the field, and both were of husbands who had rashly pronounced at once a triple *talak* and then repented.

The conditional divorce, or divorce following a *ta'alik* clause in the marriage contract, must properly come under the heading of divorce at the instigation of the husband, since it is he who agrees that divorce will ensue if he breaks such and such a clause of the contract. The most frequent *ta'alik* is that of granting one's wife the right to be divorced upon proof that she has been deserted and not maintained for a certain specified period. In the marriage contracts of a few decades ago the usual clause was, 'If I absent myself six months inland or a year at sea without supporting my wife she becomes divorced with one *talak*'. Later, in the years before the last war, this was reduced to three and six months respectively. By 1950, however, perhaps owing to faster travel, the period had been shortened simply to three months' desertion with no maintenance. It has been noted above that Shafi'i law recognizes a judicial decree of divorce for desertion without maintenance, *pasah*, but only for desertion over a period of years. This accounts for the fact that many Malays label a *ta'alik* divorce (where the clause was desertion without maintenance) improperly as *pasah*. In the late nineteenth and early twentieth century records of marriages in Singapore, the desertion *ta'alik* was not very frequent, but later it became the general rule and practice and no case was heard in 1950 of a man refusing to bind himself to it at the time of the *nikah*. Theoretically, the bride's guardian has a right to insert other clauses which could be enforced if not incompatible with Muslim law. For instance, he may ask the groom to agree that should he request his wife to follow him to a different country (thereby effectively cutting her off from her relatives), she becomes automatically divorced. Later, if the husband tries to prevail upon his wife to emigrate, she can appeal to the *kathi*, who is after due investigation entitled to register the conditional divorce pronounced by the husband on the day of the marriage contract. It was almost unknown in Singapore, however, for *ta'alik* clauses to be registered in the marriage contract other than the usual desertion *ta'alik* already referred to.[1]

We now come to divorce at the instigation of the wife. Here I wish to mention not only divorce by *khula* (the wife redeeming herself by payments to her husband, *tĕbus talak*), but divorce which in point of fact is obtained

Dictionary (Mytelene 1931) derives *China buta* from the Sanskrit, and distinguishes it as etymologically separate from *China* (a Chinese). I find, however, that Wilkinson does not explain the meaning of the Sanskrit words (*chihna*, *chihnibhuta*) and that he translates *china buta* as ' "blind Chinaman"—popular name for a muhallil. . . .'

[1] In 1924, a wealthy couple (the husband was an Arab and the wife a Bugis) were married in Singapore and there were four *ta'alik* clauses, one of which allowed the wife to seek a *ta'alik* divorce if the husband gave her a co-wife. See E. N. Taylor, 'Mohammedan Divorce by Khula'.

by the wife who seeks it, is too poor to redeem herself and obtains it by exasperating her husband to such a degree that he does in fact pronounce the *talak* as though it is he who wished to dissolve the union. It is popularly believed that Muslim women are oppressed, particularly in the realm of divorce, and there is a basis of truth in this belief. On the other hand, a woman who does not wish to continue living with her husband can find many means of making his life intolerable and leaving him no alternative but to divorce her; she could neglect her domestic duties, and become quarrelsome, for instance.[1] One traditional method among Malay women is for a wife to make a loud public scene in the course of which she uses injurious language against her husband, demanding to be set free. He is then so shamed that he has to divorce her—for how could he continue living with such a person after this? 'It is not as if she is the only woman left in the world, is it?' people comment.

There are, on the other hand, occasions when a wife rashly asks to be divorced in a fit of exasperation, and if it happens that her husband is also in an angry mood he goes to the *kathi* to repudiate her with one *talak*. Later, both repent and the *kathi* is then asked to register a revocation of the divorce. Theoretically, a Muslim can revoke the divorce he has pronounced without taking his wife's opinion into consideration. Such a procedure was rare in Singapore, however, where *kathi* usually ensured that the wife was willing to resume the union. From 1921—a date since which almost complete records of marriages and divorces are available—to 1949 the average yearly amount of *rojo* has been 7·7 per cent of the average yearly divorces.

Khula. In Singapore the most frequent payment by the wife to her husband when she seeks a *khula* divorce has been to renounce her claim to the $22.50 *mas kahwin* if it is owing, or to pay him that sum back if the amount is not outstanding. In the majority of cases the *mas kahwin* is not paid but registered as *hutang* (due) when the marriage contract is signed. On the other hand, if the couple have only recently been married and the wife seeks to dissolve the union, it is common for the man to ask for more substantial compensation before he will agree to grant the divorce. Sometimes he demands the full amount of the marriage expenses (*bĕlanja kahwin*) which he gave, and sometimes he may be content with only half that sum. If the woman seeks a divorce because she has another suitor, the latter usually agrees to pay the husband (through the intermediacy of the wife in question) twice the amount of the *bĕlanja*. I came across such a case in Penang in 1950, when a man paid $1,000 (the *bĕlanja* had been $500) to the husband of a woman he loved and wanted to marry, so that she might be divorced by *khula*. In Singapore the percentage of *khula* divorces was extremely small. I took a sample of every tenth case of divorce from the Divorce Registers of the Colony, analysed the cases, and found that in the

---

[1] Rosemary Firth, op. cit., p. 31, found this to be the case among Kelantan Malays.

course of the years 1921 to 1949 the average yearly percentage of *khula* divorces was 5·7.

Year	Sample	Khula	Year	Sample	Khula	
1921	113	16	1935	116	4	
1922	124	13	1936	119	4	
1923	121	11	1937	121	2	
1924	128	9	1938	124	7	
1925	132	4	1939	115	6	
1926	133	3	1940	124	7	
1927	147	12	1941	127	5	
1928	142	8	1942	114	11	
1929	134	7	1943	171	11	
1930	137	8	1944	*167*	9	(See note)
1931	126	14	1945	205	8	
1932	128	14	1946	173	6	
1933	126	9	1947	158	8	
1934	113	5	1948	154	11	
			1949	140	8	

NOTE

For 1944, during the Japanese occupation, 496 entries of divorce registrations are missing from the records. The exact number missing is known from the system of numbering. This fact, however, does not seriously prejudice the validity of the sample. It does mean, though, that if the records were available, the number in the sample would be increased by 50, that is 167+50. It is not possible to know the proportion of *khula* divorces for these cases.

The above figures show some variety in the annual percentages of *khula* divorces; the lowest percentages are for the years 1925, 1926 and 1937, while the highest occur in 1921, 1922, 1931 and 1932. However, it is difficult to ascertain how reliable *khula* figures are, because in some cases a couple may reach an amicable settlement as to the payment the wife will make to obtain divorce, and not mention the fact to the *kathi*, who registers the divorce as one pronounced at the will of the husband, as an ordinary *talak* divorce, and not as a *khula* divorce.

Where the entry clearly refers to *khula* divorces, the most common amount paid by the wife is $22.50 which is, of course, the conventional sum of the *mas kahwin*.

One final note about the figures is necessary. The Registers of Marriages and Divorces in the Colony from which they are taken include *all* Muslim marriages and divorces, that is Indian and Arab as well as Malay. The number of Arab and of Muslim Indian marriages is comparatively so small in the Colony, however, that it is not thought their inclusion in the records will greatly alter the significance of the conclusions reached.[1] It would

[1] The total number of Arabs returned for the Colony in 1947 was 2,591 (see Census Report for 1947, p. 8). All the Arabs are Muslims. No question was asked about religion in the 1947 Census, and it is therefore impossible to give an exact figure for Muslim Indians. In 1931 there were 13,330.

have been extremely difficult totally to exclude Indian and Arab cases, as it is not always possible to tell from the records when they occur. Only the personal names of the parties and of their fathers are usually given, and Ahmad *bin* Hassan could be Malay, Arab or Indian. In the earliest records (of the last century and of the first decade of the present one), the residence of the fathers of the parties, e.g. Singapore, India, Arabia, was given, and this practice would have been helpful for purposes of analysis had it been continued after 1909.

	Marriages	Total Number of Divorces	Rojo (Revocations)
1921	2,055	1,133	61
1922	2,073	1,239	55
1923	2,113	1,205	61
1924	3,089	1,285	60
1925	2,616	1,311	61
1926	2,633	1,335	80
1927	2,554	1,466	80
1928	2,556	1,421	76
1929	2,469	1,428	67
1930	2,307	1,366	78
1931	2,177	1,264	81
1932	2,084	1,277	96
1933	2,006	1,260	89
1934	2,163	1,132	70
1935	2,070	1,159	69
1936	2,039	1,182	94
1937	2,320	1,208	92
1938	2,065	1,241	98
1939	2,014	1,145	87
1940	2,213	1,249	111
1941	2,440	1,267	104
1942	2,949	1,139	112
1943	3,582	1,705	191
1944	2,907	2,165	225
1945	2,982	2,046	193
1946	3,095	1,734	167
1947	2,784	1,588	157
1948	2,605	1,545	222
1949	2,516	1,401	144

NOTE

For every 100 marriages registered in any one year, there are at least 50 divorces registered in the same year, 1942 and 1943 excepted; in some cases the percentage is very much higher, especially in 1944 and 1945. Revocations of divorces vary from a minimum of 4·4 per cent of the total number of divorces (in 1922) to a maximum of 14·4 per cent (in 1948), while the yearly average is 7·7 per cent.

CAUSES OF DIVORCE

It is extremely difficult to ascertain causation in divorce. Often the explicit reason is far from being the real one, and more often still there are more than one or two factors involved. Consequently one must proceed very cautiously in an examination of the material collected from documents or in the field. Conclusions reached can only be tentative. If this holds true of a sociological analysis of divorce in a Western country—where divorce proceedings are usually lengthy and involved and the parties must produce adequate evidence to support their claims—it is all the more true in an examination of the institution as far as Malays are concerned. A Malay, being a Muslim, may (and often does) pronounce a divorce without taking too much trouble to explain either to his wife or to the *kathi* the reason for his action.

I discussed at great length with my informants the grounds for divorces that had occurred in their village or district. Husbands stated that they had divorced their wives for one or more of the following causes:

1. She frequently left the conjugal home to visit her mother for long periods of time.

2. She wanted him to live in her parents' home, or to seek work in her village.

3. She was of immoral behaviour, paraded in the streets, and joked freely with men.

4. She was a bad housekeeper, always asked for more money, and wanted to spend all his earnings on herself alone.

5. She was of a quarrelsome nature and stupidly jealous.

6. Incompatibility of temperament. Neither was to blame. Perhaps a spell had been cast upon them.

7. She was cruel to his own children—her stepchildren—or short-tempered with the children of the union, and this led to frequent conjugal quarrels.

A divorced wife, if she had not instigated the proceedings either by determinedly driving her husband to repudiate her or by obtaining a *khula* divorce, gave one of the following explanations:

1. He found somebody else who was prettier or younger and he then cast her off.

2. Some enemy of hers cast a spell which suddenly caused her husband to hate her and so he repudiated her.

3. She was poor and another woman with money seduced him.

4. His mother was a wicked person; she disliked her daughter-in-law, and urged her son to repudiate her.

5. Incompatibility of temperament.

6. She was often ill and he found her a burden.

If it was a *pasah* divorce or a divorce following a desertion *ta'alik*, the cause was obvious, desertion and lack of maintenance, and the divorcée rarely troubled to state additional reasons. If it was a *khula* divorce, or if she was really the instigator by nagging her husband into repudiating her, the wife gave one or more of the following grounds:

1. He did not maintain her adequately, either because he was lazy and did not earn sufficient money; or because he spent most of what he earned on himself, or on gambling.

2. He was unfaithful to her.

3. He was of a very jealous disposition and this led to frequent and exhausting scenes; he would not let her go out at all, even to visit relatives.

4. He wanted her to live with him permanently in his native district, away from her own parents and close relatives.

5. His mother interfered too much and quarrelled with her, and he sided with his mother against his wife.

6. He was physically cruel to her or to their children, or to her children by a former marriage.

When giving one or more of the above grounds of discontent, a Malay woman often added that when her parents or her *saudara dekat* saw her plight, they encouraged her to seek a divorce, or else she might not have been bold enough to take the step without their support.

As far as adultery is concerned, whereas a woman will not admit her unfaithfulness to be the cause of the dissolution of the union, a man may occasionally state with a twinkle in his eye, 'Well, I was very naughty and liked chatting and joking with other women, so my wife got jealous and annoyed and asked me to divorce her, and I did so.'

Sterility was very rarely given by the husband or the wife as a main or even contributory cause of divorce. If a couple had no children within the first two or three years of marriage, it was customary for them to adopt the child of a prolific relative or else to buy an infant Chinese girl. They cherished the adopted child as their own.

Perhaps one of the best ways of showing how a couple arrived at a divorce is to give brief descriptions of a few of the cases I was able to investigate personally.

1. The couple were cross-cousins. The girl's parents were both dead and she lived on a small island off the coast with her maternal grandmother. Her father's sister was a widow living in Tanjong; she had several children, including a son of twenty-two years who was engaged in fishing. A marriage was arranged between the girl and this young man and there was a big wedding as this was a first occasion for both the bride and the groom. It was agreed that the couple would live on the nearby island with the bride's grandmother. Within a few weeks of the wedding, the groom's mother was constantly finding fault with her daughter-in-law. She was all the bolder in her criticisms as the girl was also her niece. The aunt was industrious and very agile while the niece was lazy and had been spoilt by her old grandmother. Soon the young woman became pregnant and found an added

excuse for lying down in the daytime or chatting with her friends. One day the husband was taken very ill and as soon as his mother heard the news she rowed over to the island in her boat, made a loud and angry scene accusing her daughter-in-law of neglecting the patient grossly, and took him back to her own home at once. She looked after him with great care, ostensibly sold some of her jewelry to get him all the medicines he might need, and complained bitterly about her niece to everybody. The young woman meanwhile was nearing confinement and she gave birth to a baby girl in her own home. Her husband's health eventually improved but he did not go back to live with her. He himself was not a very industrious fisherman, and when they had lived together he had not regularly gone out to sea, or earned enough money to support his wife adequately. Now he gave her nothing at all. Eventually he obtained employment as a policeman in town in the Extra Constabulary, and pronounced a one-*talak* divorce. She was not eager to keep the small baby and her mother-in-law therefore took it away and looked after it. The young woman never came to see the child. The general opinion in the area was that the mother-in-law was mainly to blame in the affair: she had the reputation of being a domineering and quarrelsome person. When the baby was ten months old it sickened and died. The mother was informed, but fearing a scene she did not come to the mainland, to the house of her aunt, for the funeral. A year later a marriage was arranged between this young woman and a middle-aged man working in town as a taxi-driver.

2. Salima was the eldest of three children. Her father was dead and her mother had not remarried. When the girl was fourteen she was married to a young man of twenty-three who was born in the same Singapore village but who had been brought up in the Federation and was then working in a Government department as a clerk. The match was thus a very desirable one for the girl and a few weeks after the wedding she went to live with her husband in the quarters provided for him. She was very happy in the beginning as he was kind and attentive. On the other hand, although his salary was substantial, he did not always give her sufficient money for housekeeping. Then she came to know that he gambled at cards. There was no work on Fridays and sometimes he would go straight to a club on Thursday afternoon to gamble and not come home until the early hours of Saturday morning, when he would rest for a while, and go to work. She told me: 'Often I would wait for him to come home and eat in the evening, hour after hour, and he would not come until past midnight. I had my first baby then and I was very young and inexperienced and found it trying to look after the child in the daytime and then wait in vain with the meal ready for my husband to arrive. But what used to drive me insane with rage was when, on the day he was paid his monthly salary, he would not come home but go straight to the club to gamble. I had my account at the local shop to settle and of course very often he would come home having lost all his salary, so that I had to pawn or sell my jewelry to pay our debt

at the shop. I used to lose my temper then and ask him to divorce me. My mother was not always living with me because she could not bear to see my husband behave in such a manner, so she would spend a few weeks in my house and then go back to her village, afraid lest she encourage me to ask for a divorce and then blame herself for it. He rarely won any money, but when this happened he walked proudly as if he had bought me a house. It is true that he had no other faults, he never went about with other women, having had his fill of that sort of pleasure before he married me. But I could not bear this existence much longer, with small children to support, and so I nagged him and quarrelled until he agreed to divorce me. Now I have remarried and my children are with me and although my present husband does not earn a large salary I feel happier and more secure.'

3. The couple were married when both were very young; it was a first marriage. They had seven children but only two were alive when they divorced. The husband was a semi-skilled labourer and very hard-working. The wife was pretty and coquettish. During the Japanese occupation the husband lost his job and often went to town to act as middleman in small business deals. His wife remained in the village and there she carried on a love affair with the local Indian shopkeeper. Soon her behaviour became the scandal of the district, but it took a long time for the news to reach the husband. When he did find out, however, he said nothing to his wife and decided to revenge himself as cruelly as he could. During his trips to town he had made the acquaintance of a well-to-do middle-aged couple who had a Chinese adopted daughter of marriageable age. The young man pretended that he came from the north of the Malay Peninsula and had settled in Singapore on account of his business. He brought some friends who testified to his good character, and as the couple were eager to see the girl married off (there was a strong rumour during the Occupation that the Japanese would forcibly take away all virgin girls, Malay as well as Chinese) the wedding was arranged. A few days later the husband brought home his new bride to his first wife. The older woman was enraged. She left the couple in the house and went with her children to live at her sister's home across the road. Every time she walked in the village, however, people would mutter disparaging remarks, and young boys would tease her mercilessly about having a co-wife, a *madu*. Eventually she begged her husband to divorce her and he did so, magnanimously allowing her to keep the house he had built during their marriage and the jewelry he had bought her.[1] She also retained custody of the children. He moved to a neighbouring village to settle with his new wife. Later I came to know both women well. Once I asked the younger one how she reacted when she found that her groom had grossly abused her adoptive parents' confidence by pretending he was unmarried and that Singapore was not his real home. She replied that of course she had been extremely upset, especially when she came to the house of the first wife; but when he explained matters to

[1] See below, p. 125.

her she had some sympathy for him and understood how bitter he felt towards the woman who had made him an object of ridicule by being openly unfaithful to him with a South Indian. She added: 'Besides he is handsome and clever and I was in love with him, and we were already married, so there was little I could do. Anyway he soon divorced her and we now live elsewhere. He is very hard-working, gives me enough money, so everything has ended well.' The general opinion of fellow villagers was that the first wife received what she deserved and that she was lucky to be allowed to keep the house and jewelry. She still had the house when I left the Colony, but she had long sold her jewelry in order to support herself, and she had become almost a regular prostitute.

4. A young girl of sixteen was married to a widower in his fifties. She was unhappy from the beginning but did not dare to revolt openly soon after the marriage. She grew to hate the man more and more every day. He had worked as a craftsman in a jeweller's shop and later had his own small business, and he used to lavish presents and gold ornaments upon his young wife. They had no children. She used to speak disdainfully about him and refer to him as *orang tua itu* (that old man). Within a year of the marriage she was chatting and joking with younger men in the presence of her husband in order to provoke him into divorcing her. Eventually she abused the older man in public, threw his presents and jewelry at him, and threatened to go to the *kathi* and seek a dissolution of the marriage on the (false) grounds that her husband was impotent. This threat so terrified him that he granted her request and repudiated her. She went to live in the house of her married sister and a year later she married a man of her own age.

It was rare for a marriage to endure among Singapore Malays when the disparity of ages was so great. Malays of recent Javanese immigration were particularly known to allow these unions, but in 1949 and 1950 there was a strong current of opinion against the practice. As a general rule the older man gave a larger sum for the *bělanja kahwin* than a young man might do, and he was content with a modest ceremony. Moreover, he often gave handsome presents to the girl's parents or guardians to persuade them to agree to the match. In two cases I knew of a middle-aged man marrying a young girl, the parents of the girl were heavily in debt to the older man and the union liberated them from the debt.

Rosemary Firth found that she could distinguish four main factors in divorce, from the reasons which her informants gave her. These were: 'childlessness; incompatibility; attachment to distant home and parents; and extravagances.' She adds that childlessness is not necessarily followed by divorce, unless there is one other factor as well, such as incompatibility, or the wife's desire to return home.[1] Her conclusion about causation in divorce shows some similarity btween Kelantan Malays and Singapore Malays:

[1] See Rosemary Firth, op. cit., p. 25.

'. . . incompatibility in one form or another is the basic reason for most divorces. Common situations are: jealousy of the one party at the freedom of the other in visiting coffee shops and conversing with members of the other sex; wish of one party to be free to marry someone else; and ordinary inability to adjust to each other's temperaments.'[1]

ECONOMIC ASPECTS

The economic aspects of divorce are considered under three heads: (a) the cost of the registration of the divorce, (b) the division of property, (c) the maintenance of wife and children.

(a) *The cost of the registration.* If it is the husband who wishes to repudiate his wife, the expenses are not great. He goes to the *kathi* to register the divorce and (according to the *Mohammedan Marriage and Divorce Rules*, No. 1235, issued in conjunction with the Mohammedans Ordinance) the fee for such registration is $1.00 and for a certified copy of the registration 25 cents. It was usual, however, for the man to give the *kathi* as a voluntary contribution another five dollars or so over and above this fee. He had also to pay his wife $22.50 *mas kahwin* if the amount was not paid on the day the marriage contract was signed. Sometimes the *kathi* may try to effect a reconciliation by summoning the husband and the wife to his house. In case he fails, the expenses of the divorce are a little higher because of the additional costs of transport for the parties concerned. The cost of a revocation of divorce (*rojo*) is the same as that of a registration.

For a woman who seeks to end her marriage by *pasah*, or as a result of *ta'alik*, or by *khula*, the cost of the procedure may be high. The cost of the actual registration itself remains the same as when it is a divorce pronounced by the husband, that is, $1.00. However, when the wife seeks a divorce, she must satisfy the *kathi* that her case is valid. If it is on account of desertion that she seeks a decree, she must produce proof of lack of maintenance, and the *kathi* then serves a notice upon the husband. Often, however, the husband's address is not known, and the *kathi* may then decide to serve the notice upon the husband's nearest relative, or dispense with it. Naturally some costs are involved in such a procedure, and it is the woman who must bear them. Sometimes, moreover, the husband receives the notice and chooses to appear at the hearing of the application and to deny desertion or lack of maintenance. Here more witnesses are sought, willing to make sworn statements to support the wife's or the husband's allegations, and each party pays the travelling expenses of his or her witnesses. If they live within walking distance of the *kathi*'s house, the witnesses still receive a small remuneration either in money or in gifts. In 1950, the total cost of a desertion decree for a woman might vary between $10 and $40. If the case is involved and the local *kathi* does not feel happy about deciding it himself, he seeks the advice of the Chief *Kathi* in town; expenses mount up by ten to twenty more dollars as it is customary for the applicant to pay her *kathi*'s transport expenses and offer

[1] See Rosemary Firth, op. cit., p. 26.

him compensation for the time lost on her behalf. Sometimes, also, the Chief *Kathi* asks to interview the parties and the witnesses.

Divorce by *khula* (*tĕbus talak*) is by the nature of the case usually more costly than a *pasah* or *ta'alik* divorce. It often involves considerable argument and several hearings at the *kathi*'s house; and finally when the case is settled the wife must pay her husband a certain sum of money. Often, however, he is content with the sum of the *mas kahwin*, $22.50; his wife gives it to him if she has received it in cash at the time of the wedding, or since more often the sum is still owed her, she relinquishes her right to it. However, if the wife or her family has property, or if she has a rich suitor awaiting the divorce to marry her, the husband will relinquish her only against substantial payment. Thus some cases are recorded when the price of redemption paid to the husband varied between $50 and $400. It was extremely rare for a Singapore Malay woman to pay more than this maximum, and recorded cases of payments in the region of $1,000 in the Registers of Mohammedan Divorces with few exceptions referred to other Muslim inhabitants with considerable wealth, such as Arabs.

The cost of the *khula* procedure usually varied between $20 and $60, but to this must be added the amount of money paid by the wife to the husband to redeem herself. Under the circumstances, it is not to be wondered at that over a period of years the average percentage of *khula* divorces was only 5·7.

(b) *The division of property.* In 1949 and 1950, Singapore Malays did not generally own land and with few exceptions did not work on it. Among the Malays of the Colony property mainly consisted of a small wooden house, furniture, and jewelry for the women. This was, of course, in addition to any tools of trade the men might possess.[1]

Whatever the formal cause of the divorce, whether the fault was obviously the husband's or the wife's, any property which belonged to a party before the marriage remained his or hers when the marriage was dissolved.[2] Thus if the house was built by the husband or given him by his parents before his wedding, he had an absolute right to it on his divorce. This applied, *mutatis mutandis*, to any property of the wife acquired before her marriage. On the other hand, if the house in which the couple lived was built during their married life and the furniture in it also acquired in that period, the wife had full rights to keep them if the divorce was at the will of her husband without serious provocation on her part; if, for instance, she had not deserted him or committed adultery. In such a case he left her the house, taking with him only his individual private possessions (such as clothes and personal tools), and went elsewhere to live. In 1950 I knew a husband who grew to dislike his wife intensely, but she gave him no grave grounds for divorce. On the morning on which he

---

[1] See above, pp. 37ff.
[2] cf. E. N. Taylor 'Malay Family Law'; Rosemary Firth, op. cit., pp. 33f.; and H. Subandrio, op. cit., p. 69.

decided to repudiate her, he was so angered at the thought of leaving her all their few possessions intact that he first smashed every item of crockery in the house and then pronounced the divorce.

Any property acquired during the union also remained in the possession of the wife if a divorce by *pasah* or *ta'alik* had been decreed, since in such cases it was indubitably the wife who was the injured party. When the man remarried he had to start afresh acquiring a home and household goods, unless his new partner had such property.

On the other hand, if a husband divorced his wife on account of her deserting him without great provocation, or because he had indisputable proof that she was unfaithful to him, it was she who must leave the house and property acquired by his sole earnings during marriage and go out in the clothes she stood in. The same also applied to cases where she had obtained a divorce by redeeming herself, by *khula*. The recognized principle was that in such cases, especially when she had committed adultery, she had no *adat* right to any clothes or personal jewelry which were given her by her husband during their marriage. Some informants declared that a woman repudiated for adultery had a right only to the jewels she happened to be wearing at the moment her husband pronounced the divorce, but to no others; all were agreed that she should leave behind any clothes given her by her husband, but that in point of fact she rarely did so. In this context it must be noted that the same sarong may be used by any woman, whatever her figure, since the cloth is simply gathered or folded around the waist. The husband may thus keep his divorced wife's sarongs for use by another woman he may take in marriage, or he may give them to his mother and sisters, or sell them.

Litigation concerning possession of jewelry and personal clothes was rare, as in the majority of cases the total amount did not exceed $200 and the cost of going to law might well be higher than the value of the sum involved. Most wives in fact retained after divorce the clothes and jewelry their husbands had bought them during marriage.

(c) *Maintenance of wife and children.* According to Muslim law, to *adat*, and to English law in force in the Colony the father was responsible for the maintenance of his children. If they lived with him, the matter was simple; he supported them. However, if the children went to live with their mother he rarely contributed to their upkeep,[1] and it was most unusual for his divorced wife to apply to the Courts for a maintenance order.

[1] The situation has an exact parallel in the area studied by Rosemary Firth: 'As far as consumption in relation to income is concerned the most general effect at divorce is that the burden is lightened for the man, and made heavier for the woman, since the former is normally the more important income producer . . . The burden is apt to be increased for the woman if there are young children, since they tend to stay with her. In theory, the divorced husband should contribute to their maintenance while they are young but, in practice, this seems often not to happen.' Op. cit., pp. 34-5.

After the divorce, if the father was not eager to take the children (although his wife was ready to part with them), he usually undertook to pay her a fixed sum for their keep; this varied from $5 to $20 per month per child. The man usually honoured his promise for a few months until he decided that he could no longer afford to do so, often on account of his re-marrying. Constant haggling then ensued. On the other hand, if both parents wanted to keep the children, it was common for the father to agree to leave them with their mother on condition that she assume responsibility for their maintenance.[1]

It did happen, although rarely, that a woman deserted her husband and their small children. He divorced her in due course and had to find a home for them. Ordinarily his own mother was willing to look after them, but if she was dead he asked another kinswoman to take in the children and he paid for their board. This usually meant that he bought the rice they ate, and milk if there was an infant, and he gave a few dollars in addition for other expenses such as snacks, pocket-money, etc. He also bought their clothes. Sometimes, if the burden was too great for him, the father might reluctantly give his children away in adoption, in which case he had no financial responsibility whatsoever, having transferred it to the adoptive family.

CUSTODY OF THE CHILDREN

In 1950 the law of the Colony regarding custody of the children of a divorced couple was English law.[2] The ultimate decision rested with the Civil Courts where each case was treated on its merits. Malays, however, rarely went to court on such an issue. There appeared to be no clear-cut *adat* rule concerning custody, although one principle was sometimes stated by informants: the father should keep the girls and the sons should follow their mother, for when girls reached marriageable age they needed their father as legal guardian (*wali*) to give them away, and they could also cook and keep house for him until they married; on the other hand, the sons would be able to support their mother. Other informants declared themselves to be totally ignorant of this rule or of any other. What I did observe, in practice, was that the children of a divorced couple tended to live with their mother, even when the latter remarried. The principle of the girls following their father upon their parents' divorce so that they can keep house for him seems in theory reasonable enough. In point of fact, it did not work out well for two main reasons: (a) if the girls were very small, for several years it was they who would need looking after; (b) if they were upwards of twelve or thirteen and could be of use in the house, they also needed special surveillance and chaperoning by an adult woman. Moreover, it was rare for divorced men not to remarry; and in such a case the father would no longer require the domestic services of his daughter,

---

[1] I found a similar situation in Java in 1954, in a rural area outside Djakarta.
[2] See above, p. 112.

while the latter would be unhappy with a stepmother and would return to her own mother.

Singapore Malays unhesitatingly stated that it was cruel to allow children to live with a stepmother, because however kindly a woman might be she generally ill-treated her stepchildren. It was more common to find children living with a stepfather, since the latter was away at work most of the day and had less opportunity to be unpleasant to his stepchildren.

Generally speaking, then, when a couple divorced, any small children of the union remained with their mother. The father reserved the right to see them regularly, and to have them to stay for a few days a year in his home. It was held that parents, however disreputable in behaviour, had an undisputed right of access to their children. There was also a strong belief that when a child has lived for some years with his mother, or grandmother, he becomes so attached to the person who brought him up that if parted for more than a few days from her, he pines and frets for her, is *rindu*, and may become dangerously ill as a result.[1] I once asked a young woman whether she was not worried about allowing her former husband to take away their child for a few days' visit, lest he keep it permanently. She replied confidently, 'Oh, no, for the child would surely cry and become *rindu* for me, and his father would then have to return him to me—no father wants his own child to become ill and perhaps die.'

Children who were in their teens when their parents divorced almost invariably chose to remain with their mother. There were cases, however, when a stepfather was not eager to have his wife's offspring in his home, or more frequently when her parents insisted upon bringing up her child (or children). This occurred especially when the woman was very young at the time of her divorce, had lived with her parents until her remarriage, and her mother had helped to bring up the children of the dissolved union. If the woman remarried and, particularly, if her new husband's job required her to leave her native village or district, the children continued to live with their grandparents. To live with a stepfather was a lesser evil than to live with a stepmother, but it was still an evil.

REPERCUSSIONS OF DIVORCE

So far, we have considered the institution of divorce as it affects the individuals immediately concerned. Now it is necessary to examine briefly the broader repercussions within the community: (a) one of the parties changed home, and sometimes district, (b) a breach occurred between the two groups of kin, (c) the woman, and often her children too, might become dependent upon her close kin, (d) social ostracism might be directed against the parties.

(a) *Change of residence.* Usually, the husband left the conjugal home to his wife and children, unless she had deserted him in order to follow another man or to go back to her parents. When residence during marriage

[1] See above, p. 101.

was in the native district of both parties, it was common for the husband to move away to another area either temporarily or permanently, for it was embarrassing to meet constantly soon after the divorce. Sometimes a change of residence might mean the loss of a job, but Singapore Malays did not hesitate to move in spite of this.

If residence had been in the wife's district, it was almost unknown for the divorced husband to continue to live in the area, for he had immediately become a total stranger there. Similarly, if it was the wife who had gone at marriage to live in her husband's district, she departed when she was divorced and went to her own kin.

(b) *Breach between the two groups of kin.* A divorce inevitably caused unpleasantness and strain between the two sets of close kin of the parties. Violence and loud or public quarrels hardly ever occurred in such circumstances, but the breach was not less acute because emotions were subdued. The estrangement lasted for at least three or four years, sometimes longer.

If the couple were already closely related before marriage, as in cases of cousin-marriage, there was much less restraint in the arguments and accusations which took place openly between the parents and siblings of the husband and those of the wife. On the other hand, the breach rarely lasted for more than a few months, with elderly relatives acting as mediators. The bond of consanguineous kinship was felt to be basically of supreme importance. 'Whatever happened, we are still *saudara*, we are not strangers', they explained.

(c) *Dependence of the divorced wife on her kin.* The degree of this dependence varied according to the wealth of the woman, to her ability to earn a living, and to whether she had unmarried adult sons who were willing to maintain her. However, from the moment of her divorce she was entitled to the material help and moral support of her parents, her siblings, her parents' siblings, and her first cousins, in that order, whether they did or did not approve of her divorce. Often, they might also help to support her small children. If the dissolution was at the wish of the husband without great provocation from the wife, her kin would not stint their help. If she had been largely to blame, even if she had committed adultery, they still recognized responsibility for her, although they might severely scold or even beat her for her misdemeanour. Indeed it was the only way they could behave, for it was an explicit rule that in all circumstances one must stand by a close relative in distress, especially a woman, for women are defenceless and weak.

Unless the divorced woman owned her house and lived in the same district as her close *saudara*, she usually gathered her belongings and went with her children to the home of the kinsman who would maintain her temporarily or permanently. It was rare for her *saudara* to make her a fixed money allowance. If they lived in the same area she continued to sleep with her children in her own home and went to her kinsmen for meals.

As soon as possible, however, attempts were made to find her a new husband. If this proved difficult and she was reluctant to be entirely dependent upon her kinsmen, who might themselves be very poor, she tried to earn money by taking in sewing or going into domestic service. In the rural parts one possibility was to go daily into jungle areas to gather firewood for sale to Chinese and Indian dealers. (Firewood was commonly used as cooking fuel.)

Janda had considerable freedom of movement, being fully emancipated by their first marriage, and unless in their teens and living at home with stern parents, they came and went more or less as they pleased and frequently behaved provocatively with men. Married women feared and disliked the presence of a young and attractive *janda* in their district. Malays regarded a widower or a divorcé as a suitable match for a *janda*, but they knew that these unattached and usually penurious women did not always hesitate to lure married men or young bachelors. *Janda* were rarely content with a fleeting love affair; they sought the comparative security of a legal union, and when a married man fell in love with a *janda* he usually divorced his wife and married the *janda*. The divorced wife in turn embarked upon a quest for another spouse; one broken union thus often precipitated the breakdown of other unions.

There was little prostitution by Singapore Malay women, and those who practised it were usually *janda* who had become estranged or lived away from their close kin. Sometimes if a *janda* found difficulty in remarrying and was reluctant to engage in a poorly-paid and strenuous occupation (such as gathering firewood, or preparing and hawking snacks, or laundering clothes), she might have casual affairs with men and eventually become a regular prostitute.

When she was middle-aged or elderly, the plight of a divorced woman was serious indeed if she had no close kinsman or adult children, and no hope of remarriage. Such a situation was more frequent among recent immigrants whose *saudara* were in Indonesia. These women led a pitiful existence, doing menial jobs, and frequently going hungry and ill-clad.

(d) *Social ostracism.* Divorce gave rise to a certain amount of scandal, but whatever mud there was tended to cling more to the woman than to the man. Social condemnation, amounting to ostracism, occurred in the case of a woman divorced for adultery. If her lover refused to marry her after her divorce, her guilt was not forgotten and few people welcomed any social contact with her for at least some months. She usually left the district for another locality where she was not well known and where she had kinsmen, and she stayed with them for as long as they tolerated her. If she did remarry, and then behaved irreproachably, her position became more favourable, although her friends and acquaintances did not miss many chances of referring to her past among themselves; and occasionally they made sly allusions in her presence. On the other hand, if it was the husband's adultery which had led to the dissolution of the union, allowances were made for his misdemeanour, especially if it was his first divorce. Frequent comments were, 'Well, what can you do with men, they are all very naughty!', or 'Another woman seduced him by casting a spell on him, and he was helpless.' Many women divorced for adultery also tried to excuse their actions by blaming an enemy or a lover for casting a spell upon them, but that explanation was rarely taken seriously when it came from a woman.

A man who was reputed to have been unfaithful to two or more wives in succession, or who had seduced other men's wives, was not easily forgiven. He was not welcome in most homes and parents rarely consented to give him their daughter in marriage. A divorce on account of the man's excessive jealousy or physical cruelty produced the same result. A husband was also severely blamed by the community if he exasperated his wife into demanding a divorce on account of his laziness in seeking regular employment, or because he spent whatever money he earned on gambling and other personal pastimes while his wife and children went hungry.

If a woman had been divorced more than once—whatever the circumstances—her reputation always suffered. People tended to conclude that she must have some serious defect if she could not keep two or more husbands. Even if she was clearly wronged and asked for the divorce the first time, and if it was a judicial decree granted her on account of unprovoked desertion on a subsequent occasion, the current of opinion was still not in her favour. If a third man wished to marry her he was warned by his kinsmen and friends that she had already been divorced twice and that although on the surface she might have just been unlucky, nevertheless he should not lightly enter into a union with her.

DISCUSSION

At the beginning of this chapter I posed the question, 'Do Malays regard marriage as a permanent relationship or as a partnership easily terminated?' The answer is that they hope the union will be permanent, but are fully aware of a strong possibility of its ending in divorce.

Marital status was essential for every young man in his early twenties, and every young woman in her late teens. Marriage was the mark of full adulthood; and for a woman it also meant emancipation, and freedom of movement outside the close boundaries of her parental home. It was the duty of parents to arrange for their son's or daughter's first marriage with the minimum of delay. Many Singapore Malays explicitly declared that it was better to marry off one's children when they reached a suitable age, even to unsatisfactory partners, than to let them grow older while the ideal spouse was awaited, perhaps in vain. The money spent in gifts and ceremonies and feasts at a wedding was not money given in exchange for a wife or a husband, or for any children of the union. Primarily, it was money paid for the acquisition of marital status. As we saw in an earlier chapter, the parents of the bride as well as of the groom expect to lose financially at the first marriage of their child.

Recently, conflicting theories have been discussed by social anthropologists on the subject of a correlation between high bride-price and stable unions, the material on which the discussions[1] were based being mainly African. Evans-Pritchard and Gluckman,[1] while recognizing that high marriage payment must restrict the extent of divorce, strenuously insist that the stability of marriage unions cannot be explained wholly, or even chiefly, in terms of economic motivation. In his article on the Azande, Evans-Pritchard stated:

'It is morals that censure divorce and law that refuses to recognize grounds for divorce which ensure the stability of the union of husband and wife. It derives its stability from the restraint imposed by law and morals and not from economic blackmail.'

And in *Kinship and Marriage Among the Nuer*:[2]

'. . . it can only be said that payment of bridewealth stabilizes marriage to a very limited degree.'

Gluckman,[3] quoting from the article on the Azande, comments:

'As Evans-Pritchard says, individuals when they contemplate divorce may consider difficulties about marriage payment. I suggest that this is the least important side of a complex relation. The frequency of divorce is an aspect of the durability of marriage as such, which in turn is a function of the kinship structure.'

And he adds:[4]

'It is rare divorce which allows high marriage payment, rather than high marriage payment which prevents divorce.'

These statements, in turn, have stimulated an interesting and lively discussion in the columns of *Man* on the concept of stability of marriage unions, on the need to differentiate between legal or jural bonds and conjugal relations, and on the need for defining what is meant by 'high' and by 'low' marriage payment.[5]

I propose to consider here first the question of stability and of conjugal and jural relations in marriage, and the importance of economic factors in Malay divorces in Singapore, and then to examine Gluckman's theory for any light it might throw on the Singapore Malay situation.

Stability. The position is fortunately much more clear-cut among Malays

---

[1] See E. E. Evans-Pritchard, 'The Social Character of Bride-Wealth, with Special Reference to the Azande', *Man*, 1934, 194; and *Kinship and Marriage Among the Nuer*, Oxford University Press, 1951, pp. 90-6. See also Max Gluckman, 'Kinship and Marriage among the Lozi of Northern Rhodesia and the Zulu of Natal', in *African Systems of Kinship and Marriage*.
[2] p. 91.   [3] op. cit., p. 191.   [4] ibid., p. 192.
[5] 'Bridewealth and the Stability of Marriage', *Man* 1953: 75, 122, 223, 279; 1954: 96, 97, 153. Cf. also in *Man* 1957: 59, E. R. Leach, 'Aspects of Bridewealth and Marriage Stability among the Kachin and Lakher'.

than it is among many African tribes. The conjugal and the jural bonds usually coincide, and when Malay couples have ceased to live together, with few exceptions they are also legally divorced. Among Singapore Malays there is no parallel to the Nuer situation where the same woman has legal or jural bonds of marriage with one man, and conjugal bonds with another. In exceptional cases, such as a separation without divorce, a Malay woman may have a marriage relationship which is only jural; on the other hand she almost never has a conjugal relationship with a man who is not also legally or jurally her husband.

Where the matter of statistics relating to marriage stability is concerned, I was fortunate in my investigation in that every marriage and every divorce is registered, and that records are available, with few gaps, from the end of the last century to the present day.[1]

It is necessary here to state what I mean by 'divorce rate'. As Barnes says,[2] in societies which register all marriages and divorces, 'the commonest measures are rates relating the number of divorces granted during a year or a decade to the number of marriages taking place during the same period. . . .' For instance, in Singapore in 1949 there were 2516 marriages, 1401 divorces, and 144 revocations of divorce. The divorce rate—ignoring the revocations—was 55·7 per cent. When I say that 'divorce is frequent' or 'marriage is unstable' I mean that the annual divorce percentage is around twenty or more.

Economic Deterrents. In another section of this chapter I described in detail the economic consequences of divorce as they affected the man and woman concerned. The chief point that I need repeat here is that among Singapore Malays the act of divorce entailed little immediate expense: (a) divorce procedure was usually cheap; (b) neither the husband, nor the wife, nor their kin, were involved in a costly transfer of property. No land, cattle or other capital yielding an income, and no valuables such as heirlooms, were given at marriage by the groom or his kin to the bride or her kin. The *bělanja kahwin* was not the equivalent of bridewealth; it was merely what it says, expenses for the wedding. It was not a 'consideration' given for the bride. Neither, as I said in an earlier chapter, was the *mas kahwin* bridewealth in the accepted sense, although it was translated as 'dower' by Skeat.[3] Whatever one may choose to call this payment, it is

[1] However, it is regrettable that there was usually no information about the ages of the parties, or the duration and the fertility of a marriage before divorce occurred. Neither was there any means of learning from the records the previous marital status of the groom, whether he was a bachelor, widower, divorcé, or a married man entering upon a polygynous union. As for the marital status of the bride, there was frequently an entry stating whether she was a spinster or a *janda*. However, when she was a *janda* the records did not always specify whether she was a divorcée or a widow.

[2] J. A. Barnes, 'Measures of Divorce Frequency in Simple Societies', *Journal of the Royal Anthropological Institute*, vol. lxxix, Parts I and II, 1949, published 1951.

[3] Skeat, *Malay Magic*, p. 384: 'There is a difference between *b'lanja* and *mas kahwin*, the former usually meaning the wedding expenses, the latter the dower;

necessary here to examine any role as an economic deterrent that it might have when divorce was contemplated. I have said that the *mas kahwin* was usually left unpaid by the groom at the time of marriage, but that it should be paid at once upon divorce. However, a wife might waive her right to it, and usually did so in the following sets of circumstances: (a) when it was a *khula* divorce; (b) when it was divorce by mutual consent; and (c) when she was really the instigator of the divorce (although officially it was registered as a divorce at the wish of the husband).

When it was the man only who wanted to divorce, he had to find $22.50 and this was stated by some informants to act as a deterrent. On the other hand, many asserted that a man who wanted to leave his wife but did not have, or did not wish to pay, the *mas kahwin* usually deserted her. They added that, of course, he could remarry if he wished to do so, and he could legally take as many as three other wives simultaneously. The abandoned wife could then claim a decree for desertion without maintenance but, as the procedure might well cost her more than $22.50, she often postponed taking any action. However, if she had another suitor she told her husband that she relinquished her right to the *mas kahwin* if he would divorce her, so that she too might remarry (and again have a man to support her). Thus, although in theory the owed *mas kahwin* has a deterrent effect when a man contemplates divorce, in practice this is often not so. If the *mas kahwin* was paid at marriage or shortly after, it is not returnable by the wife (except in *Khula* divorce).

It is important to note in this context that remarriage was as a rule easy and inexpensive. A divorced man usually remarried with a *janda*, and the *bĕlanja* he gave was small. The fact that he possessed no bedding or household utensils (having allowed his previous wife to keep them, as was customary) was rarely a handicap, since most *janda* had the items from their former union, and in the countryside a *janda* might also own a house. Whenever I met a man who had been widowed or divorced for some years (but was not elderly), and asked him why he did not seek a wife, the reply was invariably, 'because I have no money!' These same men, however, in a serious general discussion on marriage, often stated that if a Malay is really eager to get married he works hard and saves money, and in support of this statement they cited actual cases. Malay women also commented that if a man had set his heart on a young girl or *janda* he spent very little on himself, and saved the bulk of his earnings towards the *bĕlanja kahwin*. Consequently, there was very little pity wasted on an able-bodied man who complained that he had to endure celibacy on account of his poverty.

Finally, when a Malay had decided to repudiate his wife, as a rule he could do so without fear of being deprived either by his or her kin of food or shelter, since he was usually engaged in an occupation which made him

at least this is the Malacca terminology, which probably also obtains elsewhere.'
    The 1948 revised edition of Wilkinson's Dictionary gives for *mas kahwin* 'the settlements on a bride'.

independent economically from his own or his wife's consanguineous kins-men. As a wage earner, his source of livelihood was quite separate from his kinship links. If after his divorce his parents expressed their disapproval of his action by refusing to take him back into their home, he would easily obtain lodging and board elsewhere, since he was able to pay the required amount out of his own earnings. Even in the cases where he was dependent upon his father for his tools of trade, as when he was a fisherman and used his father's boat and tackle, he could temporarily or permanently abandon this line of employment and find paid work in town or in neighbouring areas as an unskilled labourer; unemployment was negligible in the Colony. Many Tanjong villagers who quarrelled with their father or brothers left the kampong and found jobs as labourers in R.A.F. camps or in town, or enlisted in the Special Constabulary.

In his stimulating contribution to *African Systems of Kinship and Marriage*, Gluckman contrasts the Lozi with the Zulu and advances a theory on the stability of marriage in Black Africa. The Lozi have no corporate unilineal groups of kinsmen. They do not have high marriage payment. Children belong equally to their father and to their mother, and to their paternal and maternal relatives. The Lozi have frequent divorce. The Zulu have exogamous patrilineages. They have high marriage pay-ment, and the cattle given as bridewealth transfer the woman's fertility permanently and absolutely to her husband's agnatic kin group. Divorce is rare among the Zulu. Gluckman also discusses Nuer kinship and marriage and finds that Nuer and Zulu have much in common. He states:[1]

'I have surveyed the literature on many African tribes and affirm ten-tatively that divorce is rare and difficult in those organized on a system of marked father-right, and frequent and easy to obtain in other types.'

He stresses that his hypothesis is advanced for societies with a peasant subsistence economy, and that he does 'not even venture to express an opinion on the stability of marriage in more developed communities, in towns and complex rural economies, for here many complicated variables enter.'[2] Nevertheless, I believe that his hypothesis is worth testing in more developed societies, especially when they share many points of similarity in their system of law and morals, as is the case in Malaysian societies.

It is Gluckman's proposition that stable marriage exists in 'father-right' societies while unstable marriage is found in bilateral and matrilineal societies which concerns me. While engaged in writing this study, I spent the latter half of 1954 doing fieldwork in Indonesia and tried to collect material on the stability of marriage among the Muslim people of Java (whose kinship organization closely resembles that of Singapore Malays) and among the Minangkabau of Sumatra. Marriage and divorce statistics show the people of Java to have highly unstable marriage, to much the same degree as Singapore Malays. When I looked at the comparative

[1] op. cit., p. 190.   [2] ibid., p. 206.

figures for the solidly Minangkabau area of Agam in Central Sumatra, I was struck by the contrast. My own brief field investigation in an Agam rural area had not allowed me to collect systematic information on marriage stability, but I had observed that a large proportion of young and middle-aged women in the area had never been divorced, and that marriage unions there generally appeared far more stable than they were in a village outside Djakarta where I had lived a few months earlier. Until I saw the official figures, however, I had not suspected the difference between the two general areas to be so great. In 1953 there were in Greater Djakarta 28,623 marriages, 11,706 divorces and 1,194 revocations of divorce, and in Agam 3,928 marriages, 348 divorces and 51 revocations of divorce.

Then, looking again at Gluckman's essay, I wondered whether a variation of his hypothesis might not be advanced for the Malaysian material. Where Singapore Malays, the people of Java, and the Minangkabau were concerned, marriage payment was low or negligible in all cases. The unilineal as against the bilateral principle appeared as the crucial variable, and I was prepared to put forward tentatively the hypothesis that, other things being equal, where there is unilineal descent (whether patrilineal or matrilineal), marriages are more stable. Among the Minangkabau with their exogamous matrilineages a marriage affects directly the relationships between husband's kin and wife's kin, and a divorce causes a serious breach between the two groups. This situation seemed to reinforce my hypothesis.

Meanwhile (through the very kind help of Mr J. M. Gullick, then M.C.S., who went to great trouble), I had finally obtained marriage and divorce statistics for some of the Malay States and the Settlements of Penang and Malacca. I had felt confident that the matrilineal Negri Sembilan would show their rate of divorce to be roughly in the same proportion to the divorce rates of the bilateral Malay States and the Singapore Malays, as the Agam divorce rate was to the bilateral people of Java. They did not, and of course my tentative hypothesis at once collapsed.

The Agam divorce rate was less than 10 per cent in 1953, whereas the lowest for Java was the Greater Djakarta rate of 40·9 per cent. The highest rate that year for all the Provinces of Java was for West Java: 61 per cent. In all these compilations I have ignored revocations of divorce because I was unable to obtain the relevant figures for five Malay States, including Negri Sembilan.

MUSLIM MARRIAGES AND DIVORCES IN JAVA, 1953

Area	Marriages	Divorces	Revocations
West Java	355,170	217,237	17,763
East Java	451,898	243,163	37,613
Central Java	376,490	187,834	11,433
Greater Djakarta	28,623	11,706	1,194
Jogjakarta Area	30,933	11,796	460

MUSLIM MARRIAGES AND DIVORCES IN ALL INDONESIA

	Marriages	Divorces	Revocations
1947	552,488	321,080	18,775
1948	224,436	125,942	8,584
1949	849,261	451,321	27,053
1950	1,308,480	636,249	44,109
1951	1,463,006	803,893	60,892
1952	1,305,254	780,162	59,386
1953	1,416,483	723,009	76,014

MUSLIM MARRIAGES AND DIVORCES IN MALAYA

	PERAK		NEGRI SEMBILAN	
	Marriages	Divorces	Marriages	Divorces
1945	5,047	3,203	2,039	1,710
1946	4,382	3,072	2,268	1,858
1947	4,532	2,806	2,276	1,552
1948	6,015	2,645	2,652	1,054
1949	5,803	3,020	2,615	1,527
1950	6,214	2,731	2,683	1,412
1951	6,492	2,853	2,979	1,552
1952	5,416	2,673	2,452	1,264
1953	5,172	2,464	2,114	1,036

	SELANGOR		KEDAH		PERLIS	
	Marriages	Divorces	Marriages	Divorces	Marriages	Divorces
1948			7,724	5,032	968	615
1949	3,147	1,080	7,222	4,645	962	645
1950	3,040	1,068	8,945	5,170	1,246	733
1951	3,378	1,066	9,621	4,977	1,065	845
1952	2,783	1,063	7,266	4,801	918	851
1953	2,906	1,023	6,778	4,285	834	636

	PENANG			MALACCA		
	Marriages	Divorces	Revocations	Marriages	Divorces	Revocations
1945	2,081	1,477	313	2,793	1,699	216
1946	2,216	1,402	242	1,936	993	87
1947	2,176	1,248	193	1,859	759	75
1948	2,330	1,149	85	1,767	711	52
1949	2,232	1,081	164	1,924	670	66
1950	2,676	1,102	203	2,159	729	78
1951	3,143	1,116	211	2,693	805	100
1952	2,469	1,118	225	2,235	633	77
1953	2,049	975	119	1,943	648	70

The average annual rate of divorce over nine years (1945-53) in Negri Sembilan was 59 per cent, thus showing great similarity to the situation in Singapore (56 per cent over the last nine years for which I have complete records, 1941-9). The Negri Sembilan average annual rate was higher than that of neighbouring Selangor (34 per cent), and Malacca (40 per cent); and also higher than that of Penang (50 per cent), or Perak (52 per cent). Indeed only Perlis and Kedah (of all the Malay States for which I was able to obtain figures) show a higher rate than that of Negri Sembilan, with Perlis beating all known records in the Malaysian world with a divorce rate of 92·7 per cent in 1952.

I cannot make here any serious attempt at explaining why the Minangkabau of Sumatra and of Negri Sembilan offer such a contrast in the field of marriage stability. I have not sufficient information on recent conditions in Negri Sembilan.

One obvious point about the high frequency of divorce in the Malaysian world in general was the role of Islam. I looked at the position of a Middle Eastern Muslim country, Egypt. The figures for Muslims there also show frequent divorce:[1]

EGYPT

	Marriages	Divorces	Revocations
1945	259,445	79,648	10,452
1946	270,322	80,044	10,827
1947	244,548	75,104	10,125
1948	251,732	75,709	9,595
1949	259,688	75,381	9,166

Could it be that with few exceptions (such as the Agam region of Sumatra), wherever there is Islam, and whatever the variations in kinship and social organization, there is also marriage instability? Had Islam, wherever it had gone, brought with it a system of law and morals which allows ease as well as frequency of divorce, in spite of assertions by ulema and modern apologists who stress that divorce is 'abhorred' by 'true' Muslims? The answer is, of course, that Islam permits divorce but that stable marriage in Muslim societies is not unusual.

In the Palestinian village of Artas, divorce is rare. 'Of 264 marriages 11 or 4·1 per cent were dissolved by divorce.'[2] Bride price is high, and paid to the woman's kin. It is a 'father-right' society with children belonging to their father's lineage and residing in their father's house. When divorce occurs at the wife's request, her kinsmen must return the bride price given for her. When it occurs at the husband's wish (and without grave provocation) he forfeits the bride price, and if he wishes to remarry must find

---

[1] Egyptian Government, Ministry of Finance Statistical Department, *Vital Statistics*, 1945, 1946, 1947, 1948, 1949, published respectively 1950, 1951, 1952, 1952, 1953. See also H. Ammar, *Growing Up In An Egyptian Village*, pp. 199-200, for the distribution of divorce over durations of marriage.

[2] Granqvist, op. cit., vol. 2, p. 268.

another sum. Marriage, even with a widow or divorcée, involves high expenditure (although the bride price given for a widow or a divorcée is lower than that given for a virgin). In such a society, the economic deterrents to divorce are obviously high. Granqvist states:[1]

'As far as I can see, the economic loss is greater for a man who desires divorce than it is for a woman, i.e. her own people or family (*ahel*), if it is she —or they—who desires the divorce. A woman's relatives have to give back the bride price, but instead they get back their daughter, whom they can remarry for a new bride price. The husband loses the bride price, which he has given for his wife, without getting anything instead. If he has already almost ruined himself to get his first wife or got her only with the help of his relatives, he will be careful not to divorce her without a cause. Not often is a man in a position to procure a new wife in place of her whom he has allowed to go.'

It is clear that the economic deterrent is higher for the man than it is for the woman or her kin, but I think that Granqvist argues wrongly in this statement if she implies that the economic deterrent is slight in the case of the wife. Firstly, her kin must at once find the bride price to return to her husband, whereas there is usually some delay until they are approached by a new suitor and acquire another amount from him. Secondly, the bride price they get for her as a divorcée is appreciably lower than that which they had received (and must now repay) for her as a maiden, as Granqvist herself says elsewhere.[2] Thirdly, if she is no longer young or attractive she would presumably not be desirable as a prospective bride.

Finally, there is one other important deterrent to divorce for a woman in Artas: she is parted from her children, who cannot be taken away from their father's house. Moreover, if she has sons, she forfeits the secure future which would have awaited her as the woman of authority in her household with daughters-in-law and grandchildren deferring to her. It is economic as well as emotional security. Granqvist stresses that this last factor plays a very important role in the decision some Artas widows take to remain in their dead husband's house instead of returning to their own paternal home.[3] It may well be, also, a factor which influences a mother to bear with her present conjugal unhappiness rather than seek a divorce. Indeed Granqvist hints at this in the final paragraph of her Chapter on Divorce.[4]

'The worst for a woman is that by divorce she loses her children, who belong to her husband and may not be taken away from his house. We shall in the next chapter find that this is the central question also in the natural separation and dissolution of marriage, which occurs through death.'

In Artas both Islam and general morality permit divorce. On the other hand, there are powerful economic deterrents to divorce for a man; while

[1] ibid., pp. 283-4.   [2] op. cit., vol. 1, pp. 120-1.
[3] op. cit., vol. 2, pp. 319-24.   [4] ibid., p. 287.

for a woman there is the strong deterrent of losing her children and the other deterrent of some economic loss for her paternal kinsmen.

Few social anthropologists would argue with Evans-Pritchard's and Gluckman's contention that the question of stability of marriage must always be studied within the whole context of the norms of a society. However, although economic motivation cannot always be said to be of primary importance, I doubt whether it is theoretically sound to go to the other extreme and relegate it to a negligible position. Expressions such as 'economic blackmail' are heavily charged with our own value judgments. In the Malay situation in Singapore I think it would be rash to attempt to explain away marriage instability largely in economic terms, although the lack of a powerful economic deterrent to divorce indubitably does make it easier in practice to dissolve a conjugal union; there is not sufficient evidence to decide which came first, unimportant economic deterrents or instability of marriage.

Where the broad issue of a possible correlation between marriage stability and type of kinship organization is concerned, the data on the Malaysian world and on Egypt and the Palestinian Arabs are inconclusive. All these Muslim societies have a system of law and morals which permits divorce. However, of the two patrilineal Middle Eastern societies, one has stable and the other has unstable marriage. Of the two matrilineal Malaysian societies (one of which, Negri Sembilan, is a fairly recent offshoot of the other), one has high divorce frequency and the other has not. As for the bilateral peoples of Java, the Malay Peninsula, and Singapore—all of whom have unstable marriage—the variations in their respective divorce rates are sufficiently large to make it difficult to treat them as an undifferentiated group.

Among Singapore Malays, several factors exist which are congruent with divorce frequency:

1. Law facilitates divorce, and general morality tolerates it.
2. The economic deterrents to divorce are not strong.
3. Remarriage is easy and inexpensive.
4. After her divorce, a woman can rely on her close kin for practical and moral support.
5. There is freedom of access to the children by both father and mother, and their respective kin.
6. The mechanism of adoption is available, if neither parent desires to keep the children.

I now turn to the narrower field of the emotional consequences of divorce on the children of dissolved unions. The high frequency of Malay divorce means that a large proportion of Malay children are suddenly deprived of one parent (or of both when as a result of the divorce they are placed in foster homes or given away in adoption), that their loyalties may become divided, and that they have to accustom themselves to the situation which arises when the parent with whom they live remarries and a stranger with a large share of authority is introduced in the home. So far, however, there is no adequate information to warrant the assumption (generally made for Western societies) that broken homes necessarily have an adverse effect on children's personalities among Singapore Malays. Whereas broken homes are the tragic exception in Western countries, they are common in Malay society and the children of a divorced couple are not considered special objects of pity or concern. If there is any indication that a child is unhappy because he pines for the absent parent, he is sent to live with him or her for a few days, and as a general rule his permanent residence will be determined according to his own expressed wishes. The personal happiness of the child, and not the convenience of the parents, is held by Malays to be of supreme importance.

In the European context the child of a divorced couple is usually considered a greater object of pity than the child of a happily married couple who reside permanently abroad (as in a Colony), and entrust the boy or the girl to the care of a boarding school or a guardian. In the latter case, the child sees his own father and mother at most once a year, and often only every three years. Yet a child living away from both parents is likely to be much more 'deprived' of affection than a child living with either his own father or his own mother. Obviously, it is not so much the actual emotional handicap of living away from one parent as the whole complex of attitudes about divorce and broken homes which is the operative factor in the Western situation.

Phrases such as 'the sanctity of the home', 'the sacred bond of marriage' or the moral and emotional content they carry, have no equivalent in Singapore Malay culture. No such expressions are used, and certainly the bond of marriage is not considered sacred. I saw no evidence of great moral pressure being exercised by *kathi* or by religious teachers to dissuade wives from claiming a divorce or husbands from pronouncing it. In the few cases where a woman had been living for many years with her first husband, her pride in the fact appeared to be due as much to the chastity and equanimity which were implicit in her not having sought other unions, as to the triumph of a woman who had achieved a feat rare in her community. This does not mean that the majority of Malays view the dissolution of marriage with total unconcern, only that they accept the situation with resignation.

Singapore Malays above all value harmony in personal intimate relationships. When a marriage union fails to produce even a small measure of emotional contentment and causes strife and anxiety, they find divorce the most obvious solution to their problem. Material considerations, such as economic security, are usually of secondary importance.

7

Conclusion

BOTH during the period of fieldwork and later while analysing the material collected, my chief focus of interest was the instability of marriage unions, an instability which is not a sudden development in the Colony but a characteristic of at least several decades. The majority of Singapore Malays viewed with resignation the high frequency of divorce, probably because it was a permanent feature of their society.

In 1949 and 1950, however, Muslim leaders in the Island and Malay women's associations were asking for reform in the field of marriage and divorce. Muslim divorce statistics were widely publicized in the local press; prominent Arabs, Indians, and Malays were interviewed for their opinion and they expressed great concern. Many suggestions were made and discussed by Muslims in both men's and women's formal gatherings, and in the columns of English and Malay newspapers in the Colony. Some asserted that a Malay girl's youth and inexperience at the time of marriage made her an irresponsible and irritating housekeeper, and accounted for the breakdown of many first marriages. Others stated that parents sometimes failed to ensure that the couple to be married were well suited, as when a bride in her teens was given to a middle-aged or elderly groom. Others, again, declared that a *kathi* should particularly ascertain that a girl's consent to a match was freely given, because a forced union is rarely permanent. On the other hand, some members of the Singapore Muslim Advisory Board thought it at least as important to ensure that marriages were not lightly dissolved. In public statements in 1949 and 1950 they said that it was desirable to set up an official reconciliation machinery, and urged that when a divorce was contemplated the couple should consult with the Board, who would attempt reconciliation. They added that since Singapore *kathi* appeared unable to exert sufficient pressure to prevent divorces, the Board should take action.

In Chapter 2 on Kinship we saw that Singapore Malays formally stated that an individual's paternal kinsmen were 'more important' or 'stronger' than maternal kinsmen, and that this ideology was closely bound up with Islam, but that in practice there was a definite bias in favour of maternal kin. This bias was reinforced by the fact that the children of divorced couples tended to remain with their mother.

The Singapore Malay situation has similarities with working-class

London. Young, writing in *Man*,[1] stated that among the working-classes of East London the strongest operative kinship ties are between a woman, her married children, and her daughters' children. He found that when a girl marries she usually lives either in her mother's home or near by, and that what he calls the 'matrilateral extended family' has 'economic, recreational, ceremonial and mutual-aid functions of great importance'. He believes that owing to the insecurity which working-class women had to endure until recently (on account of frequent wars, unemployment, wage-earner's risk, desertion by husbands, etc.) and to the 'resulting very high frequency of broken homes', the ties between a woman and her family of birth have been strengthened, and he thinks that these conditions may be also true of the working-classes of most industrial countries.

I would go further and state that in all societies where marriage relationships are unstable, and whatever the economy, one may expect to find a high degree of emotional and economic solidarity between a woman and her close kinsmen. However, where the child of a dissolved union is concerned, his position will be determined in the first place according to the nature of the kinship system. In societies with corporate unilineal groups the child's alignment, at least legally, is clear. On the other hand, if the kinship system is bilateral—as among Malaysians of Singapore, Malaya and Java, as well as among the English—the tendency, so far as we know, is for children of divorced couples to be closely bound to their mother and to her kinsmen and to have only an attenuated link with their father's kinsmen.

This leads me to an assessment of the status of women among Singapore Malays. Given a society where until two or three decades ago education was largely restricted to the male sex, where women could be divorced at the will of their husbands and left without maintenance, and where it was not traditional for women to be gainfully occupied, one would expect to find considerable subservience by adult women to the will of their husbands or of the men of their own kin group. In point of fact, however, I found that in almost every field of household activity a wife had at least as much authority as her husband, and frequently more. Although divorce meant serious hardship for the majority of women, they adopted a firm attitude *vis-à-vis* their husbands when the latter threatened them with it, and in conjugal arguments seldom yielded before the threat.

In general discussions, as well as in considerations of specific cases, Malay women stated that they prefer to live on inadequate and infrequent meals rather than to remain married to a man who gives them ample housekeeping money and who treats them well but whom they have grown to dislike strongly. Again and again divorced women and others discussing the position declared: 'What use is a full belly when the heart is sad?'

[1] Michael Young, 'Kinship and Family in East London', *Man* 1954, 210. See also M. Young and P. Willmott, *Family and Kinship in East London*, London 1957, especially pp. 28-67.

The fact that a woman can always depend upon her own kin's support is, of course, largely responsible for the degree of independence she shows in her conjugal relationships. On the other hand, the practical and moral help a divorced woman receives from her own relatives, especially financial help from her father and brothers, does not result in her adopting towards them an attitude of unquestioning deference and obedience in return. It is simply the duty of men to give food and shelter to their daughter or sister after she has ceased to live with her husband, even if they disapprove of the divorce which she may have sought herself. When the woman has no children the burden will be lighter to bear than when she brings young dependents with her, but whatever the circumstances a woman's kinsmen must behave as graciously as possible. If both her parents are alive a divorcée has little to worry about; she is always welcome in the household where her mother is in charge of the housekeeping.

There is also a strong tradition among Malays to protect women and to behave kindly towards them. When I discussed the role of women with Singapore Malays, they frequently declared that because women are not usually capable of earning a living, and because a woman's movements are more restricted than a man's, it was essential that men behave considerately towards women. One expression often used in this context was *pĕrĕmpuan kaki pĕndek*, women have short legs. It was explained to me that if a father scolded his sons or behaved harshly to them, the boys could leave the house and find alternative accommodation elsewhere; men can always fend for themselves; for women it was much more difficult, and therefore women were entitled to more consideration. In general, personal relationships among Malays are characterized by great restraint of behaviour and by a profound respect for individuality. The element of force or compulsion is very slight, even in the parent-child relationship.

I now turn to another principle of Malay social organization in Singapore, the solidarity between an individual and his kinsmen. In the Introduction I stated that since the Colony's Malays have little effective community organization, and no tribal, clan, or lineage organization whatever, it was important to determine the extent—if any—of formal economic solidarity among kinsmen. In Chapter 2 on Kinship we saw that there is in fact considerable solidarity (emotional as well as economic) between an individual and his close kinsmen. In Malay economic relationships in Singapore there are two apparently conflicting factors at work: individualism reflected in the way a man earns his living and acquires and manages his property, as well as in the absence of business partnerships; and interdependence among close kinsmen as evidenced by the right an individual has to appeal to a wide circle of *saudara* for financial help or for their services whenever he is in distress. We saw further that these two factors are not in fact incompatible. Firstly, a Malay in need appeals to his kinsmen not as to a corporate group (which in any case does not exist), but on a person-to-person basis, and he does not expect help to be automatically forthcoming. Secondly, it is because of the lack of joint ownership and exploitation of property, and because of the fact that individual wage-earning is the basis of Malay economy in the Colony, that there is the need to have a range of persons to whom one can go in a crisis. Theoretically, these persons might be selected on the basis of friendship, or of similarity of occupation or residence; and indeed for one specific purpose, that of death-benefits, Malays do come into association on such a basis. Death-benefit societies provide a solution to the urgent, and often sudden, need for obtaining a large sum of money within a few hours. However, where a more enduring and complex relationship of interdependence is concerned, Singapore Malays turn to the more 'natural' link of kinship. The basic differentiation between people is that between *saudara* and *orang lain*, and among the former it is the general rule to expect sympathy and help in all spheres, while among the latter the most one can hope for is neutrality.

Among *saudara* the strongest operative tie is of course between parents and children, and it is in this relationship that the most interesting pattern of rights and duties manifests itself. Parents must be forever ready and willing to help their children in every way (even after they have married and settled in independent residences), and they expect little in return. In principle and in practice there is only slight respect for old age, and a man is always expected to consider his own wife and children's welfare before that of his parents. An elderly couple, unless they are infirm, must attempt to earn their living, and even if in the past they have shown great generosity toward their sons and daughters, they do not believe themselves entitled to regular financial help in return. In other words, there is hardly any personal reciprocity between parents and children: for the former it is always more blessed to give than to receive.

However hard husband and wife may have worked to accumulate furniture, jewelry, and other possessions, and although by custom and by law the goods they have acquired remain their exclusive property, they would consider themselves unnatural parents if they enjoyed some material comforts in their old age while their adult children were struggling along without any economic help from them. The situation is not as unfair to the old couple as might appear at first sight, for they in their youth would have had the same type of relationship with their own parents. Elderly informants had much to say about changing conditions in the Colony, but never did any of them state that the adult children of today differed in their attitude to their old fathers and mothers from the adult children of past generations. One gives to one's children all the privileges which one had received from one's own parents several decades earlier, and although there is no direct personal reciprocity between parent and child, there is what for want of a better term I call 'indirect generation reciprocity'.

Among other categories of close kin, however, between siblings, first cousins, and parent's sibling and sibling's child, direct reciprocal relations are more common.

In the Introduction I stated that the institution of the adoption of children was an integral part of Malay family organization in Singapore, because I believe that if it did not exist several aspects of family organization would be different. Firstly, sterile unions would be frequently dissolved by divorce, whereas at present adoption provides a remedy. Secondly, divorced and widowed persons would find remarriage more difficult if they had no alternative to keeping in their new home their children by a former union. Thirdly, illegitimate children and the children of destitute people might be abandoned, or allowed to starve, or placed in orphanages, instead of being welcome as they now are in other Malay homes. Finally, childless Malay couples would, in their old age, be deprived of the measure of security which their adopted children now give them when they grow up.

In all societies there are, on the one hand, couples who want children but who cannot beget them, and on the other hand, couples who beget children whom they do not want or whom they cannot adequately maintain. In few societies, however, is the problem as neatly resolved as in Singapore Malay society, and with such a minimum of personal unhappiness to either the parents or the children concerned. The transfer of children from homes into which they are born, and where for a variety of reasons they cannot remain, to homes which are ready to welcome them and care for them, takes place without great formality and usually with the understanding that the welfare of the children will always be of paramount importance to the adopting parents.

There are exceptions to this happy state of affairs, however. In some cases, orphaned or destitute children are taken in by a close kinsman mainly out of a sense of duty, and are brought up with little kindness or consideration; while in other cases a girl may be taken in adoption to serve as unpaid housemaid. There is also another practice—that of temporary or conditional adoption—which sometimes leads to much misery and heartbreak for either the child or the adoptive parents concerned. This occurs most frequently in the case of an orphan or of the child of a destitute widow or divorcée, when the boy or girl is past early infancy and is taken on trial in a new home: he or she is old enough to feel uprooted by the sudden change and may not settle down. Fortunately, however, the incidence of unsuccessful adoptions is comparatively small.

Throughout the past chapters I have stressed the importance which Singapore Malays attach to personal happiness. It would be difficult to over-emphasize this attitude: it permeates all fields of human behaviour. When a Malay contemplates a change of residence, marriage, divorce, or the exercise of a profession, the primary consideration is not so much the material advantages to be gained as the serenity of mind which the new type of existence is likely to yield. It is not, of course, that earthly pleasures and worldly goods are despised, or that Malays believe that there is inherent good in renunciation. I could find no evidence whatever that asceticism, even in a mild form, was valued for its own sake or as a means of attaining spiritual joy. On the contrary, the stress was always on gathering rosebuds while one may and on leading as leisurely a life as possible. Singapore Malays, being Muslims, believe in an after-life (*akhirat*), but their conception of divine retribution is hazy. The majority of them appear to think that if they have committed no major sin, such as murder, and if they are given a proper Muslim burial, their souls will rest in peace.

Every individual has a right to attain personal happiness by all legal means, and no one is expected to forgo this right lightly. Of course, the interests of the various members of a group of kin (and more frequently of husband and wife) may, and do, clash. A man prefers to work shorter hours and earn less money, but his wife may suffer as a consequence since she will receive from him a reduced sum for housekeeping, clothes and luxuries. A woman wants to continue living with her mother in her native village, but her husband is reluctant to do so because he has to travel a long distance to get to his place of work, and therefore he insists on a change of residence. Obviously, adjustments have to be made if the marriage is to endure. However, there is no basic assumption that marriages must be preserved because divorce is evil. It is friction and incompatibility in intimate relationships which are bad: they cause anxiety and 'restlessness of heart' (*hati tidak sĕnang*), and there can be little worse harm than this.

When the happiness of adults conflicts with that of a young child, as when the latter is transferred in childhood but pines for his former home, the adults are in duty bound to yield to the child, and to allow him to live where he pleases, even if they are convinced that his permanent transfer to the adoptive parents would ensure a much more secure future for him. This type of situation exemplifies two distinct sets of attitudes: one is that the well-being of young children is more important than the convenience or welfare of adults, and the other that immediate emotional security or contentment is more important than the prospect of practical advantages in the years ahead.

What of the future? In 1950 there were several trends in the Colony which might lead to significant repercussions on Malay kinship organization. There was the growth of female education; the insistence on reform in the field of divorce; the active desire on the part of young men to find secure employment; and the increasing range of social services and social welfare.

The growth of female education may lead an increasing number of young girls to seek paid employment outside the home and to attain a measure of emancipation from parental authority. Further, a young woman who can earn a living in better-paid occupations than the traditional ones of making and selling food snacks, and domestic service, will have more assurance in conjugal arguments. It is probable that her financial independence will allow her to contemplate divorce without the alarm which an uneducated woman, especially when she had several small children, felt in 1949 and 1950.

As for reform in the field of divorce, by 1950 the proposals put forward were not of a revolutionary nature but had mainly urged more care in the arrangement of first marriages and recommended the setting up of an official reconciliation machinery. It seemed likely, however, that agitation and proposed free legal advice by women's welfare societies would eventually lead divorcées to take advantage of the existing legislation by which a divorced man could be compelled to pay maintenance for his children. Once a Singapore Malay knows that he cannot avoid all the economic responsibilities of parenthood simply by pronouncing a divorce formula, and that if he remarries he will have to support his children by a former union as well as his new wife, it may be that he will hesitate before deciding to repudiate the woman who has borne him children. Thus any likelihood that advanced education for girls might lead to their acquiring financial independence, and in turn that such independence would indirectly lead them to be less patient in matrimonial disputes and to raise the divorce rate, could be counteracted by the restraint men would show in pronouncing a divorce when they had young children to maintain.

The 1950 provisions for free education in English, and the campaign by Malay leaders in the Peninsula and in the Colony to urge young boys to be industrious and ambitious students and to compete with Chinese and Indians on terms of equality for Government and commercial posts, seemed likely to result in a growing number of young Singapore Malays in stable and well-paid employment. The occupations of fishing, unskilled and casual labour, rubber-tapping, and others which yield a small and uncertain income will probably attract fewer recruits from the younger generation.

If in future decades the Malay community of the Island becomes more prosperous, and if the majority of the men are in stable employment and have the prospect of a secure future, one effect of the change may be to lessen the need for economic solidarity among close kin.

The sharp increase in the scope of social services since the end of the war might be another factor in diminishing this economic solidarity. Already in 1950 some Malays suffering from a chronic and incapacitating disease—such as tuberculosis—were in receipt of a regular financial allowance from Social Welfare funds. A few years earlier such men and their wives and small children would have been largely dependent upon the help of their *saudara děkat*.

The fact that Singapore Malays will probably become more self-reliant financially need not mean that they will, as a result, be less eager to seek the advice, the friendship, and the company of their kinsmen. On the contrary, it is just as likely that relationships between kin will benefit from the absence of strain which tends to arise when some individuals are an economic liability to others.

List of Works Cited

ABDULLAH, *Hikajat Abdullah*, edited by R. A. Datoek Besar and R. Roolvink, Djakarta and Amsterdam 1954.

Adatrechtbundels, vol. xxvi, *Maleisch Gebied en Borneo*, The Hague 1926.

AMEER ALI, *Mahommedan Law*, Calcutta 1929.

AMMAR, HAMED, *Growing Up In An Egyptian Village*, London 1954.

BARNES, J. A. 'Measures of Divorce Frequency in Simple Societies', *Journal of the Royal Anthropological Institute*, vol. lxxix, Parts I and II 1949, published 1951.

BLUNT, W. S., *The Future of Islam*, London 1882.

BROWN, C. C., *Malay Sayings*, London 1951.

BUCKLEY, C. B., *An Anecdotal History of Old Times In Singapore*, 2 vols., Singapore 1902.

Colony of Singapore Annual Report, 1949, Singapore, 1950.

DEL TUFO, M. V., *A Report on the 1947 Census of Population, Malaya*, London and Singapore 1950.

DENNYS, N. B., *A Descriptive Dictionary of British Malaya*, London 1894.

DJAMOUR, J., 'Adoption of Children Among Singapore Malaysians', *Journal of the Royal Anthropological Institute*, vol. lxxxii, Part II, 1952.

EVANS-PRITCHARD, E. E., 'The Social Character of Bride-Wealth, with Special Reference to the Azande', *Man*, article 194, 1934.

— *Kinship and Marriage Among the Nuer*, London 1951.

FIRTH, RAYMOND, *Malay Fishermen: Their Peasant Economy*, London 1946.

— *Report on Social Science Research in Malaya*, Singapore 1948.

FIRTH, ROSEMARY, *Housekeeping Among Malay Peasants*, London 1943.

FREEDMAN, MAURICE, *Chinese Family and Marriage in Singapore*, London 1957.

GEDDES, W. R., *The Land Dayaks of Sarawak*, London 1954.

GIMLETTE, J. D., *Malay Poisons and Charm Cures*, London 1915.

GRANQVIST, H., *Marriage Conditions in a Palestinian Village*, 2 vols., Helsingfors, vol. 1, 1931; vol. 2, 1935.

JOSSELIN DE JONG, P. E. de, *Minangkabau and Negri Sembilan, Socio-Political Structure in Indonesia*, Leiden 1951.

LANG, OLGA, *Chinese Family and Society*, New Haven 1946.

LEACH, E. R., *Social Science Research in Sarawak*, London 1950.

— 'Aspects of Bridewealth and Marriage Stability Among the Kachin and Lakher', *Man*, article 59, 1957.

LEVY, R., *An Introduction to the Sociology of Islam*, 2 vols., London 1931.

MCELWAINE, P., *Revised Edition of the Laws of the Straits Settlements*, Singapore 1936.

MAKEPEACE, W., BROOKE, G. E. and BRADDELL, ST. J., editors, *One Hundred Years of Singapore*, 2 vols., London 1921.

MORRIS, H. S., *Report on a Melanau Sago-Producing Community in Sarawak*, London 1953.

MOUBRAY, G. A. de C. de, *Matriarchy in the Malay Peninsula*, London 1931.

NAWAWI, *Minhaj Et Talibin*, translated by E. C. Howard from the French ed. of L. W. C. Van Den Berg, London 1914.

RADCLIFFE-BROWN, A. R. and FORDE, DARYLL, editors, *African Systems of Kinship and Marriage*, London 1950.

RADCLIFFE-BROWN, A. R., *Structure and Function in Primitive Society*, London 1952.

SALE, G., *The Koran, Translated from the Original Arabic*, London, n.d.

SCHNEIDER, D. M., 'A Note on Bridewealth and the Stability of Marriage', *Man*, article 75, 1953.

SKEAT, W. W., *Malay Magic*, London 1900.

SNOUCK HURGRONJE, C., *The Achehnese*, 2 vols., trans. A. W. S. O'Sullivan, Leyden 1906.

SOCIAL WELFARE DEPARTMENT, SINGAPORE, *Social Survey of Singapore 1947*, Singapore 1948.

SUBANDRIO, H., *Javanese Peasant Life, Villages in East Java*, Unpublished thesis, Academic Post-Graduate Diploma in Anthropology, University of London 1951.

SWETTENHAM, F. A., *British Malaya*, London 1948.

TAYLOR, E. N., 'Malay Family Law', *Journal of the Royal Asiatic Society, Malayan Branch*, vol. xv, Part I, 1937.

— 'Mohammedan Divorce by Khula', *Journal of the Royal Asiatic Society, Malayan Branch*, vol. xxi, Part II, 1948.

VESEY-FITZGERALD, S., *Muhammadan Law, An Abridgement According to its Various Schools*, London 1931.

VLIELAND, C. A., *British Malaya, A Report on the 1931 Census*, London 1932.

WILKINSON, R. J., *Life and Customs, Part I, The Incidents of Malay Life*, Papers on Malay Subjects, Kuala Lumpur 1908.

— *The Peninsular Malays, Part I, Malay Beliefs*, London 1906.

— *Law, Part I, An Introductory Sketch*, in *Papers on Malay Subjects*, Kuala Lumpur 1908.

— *A Malay-English Dictionary (Romanized)*, 2 vols., Mytilene 1932.

— *An Abridged Malay-English Dictionary (Romanized)*, 7th edition, London 1948.

WINSTEDT, R. O., *The Malays, A Cultural History*, London 1950.

— *The Malay Magician*, London 1951.

YOUNG, MICHAEL, 'Kinship and Family in East London', *Man*, article 210, 1954.

YOUNG, M. and WILLMOTT, P., *Family and Kinship in East London*, London 1957.

YVAN, DR, *Six Months Among the Malays and a Year in China*, London 1855.

Index

Abortion, 88f.
Adat, 13ff., 40, 68f.
Adoption, 2, 30f., 41, 92ff., 145; of Chinese children, 98ff.; nominal, 94; temporary, 95f.; total, 96ff.
Affines, 24, 26, 29f.
Age-structure, 4
Ameer Ali, Sayed, 112n.
Ammar, Hamed, 102n., 137n.
Anak angkat, 30f., 93ff.
Anak dara, 68, 72, 78f., 81
Arabs, 2, 6n., 10, 11, 13, 15, 17ff., 21, 116n.
Associations, voluntary, 17, 19, 21, 22, 47

Bangsa, 12
Barnes, J. A., 132
Běla kampong, 20f.
Bělanja kahwin, see Marriage expenses
Běrsanding, 76
Besan, 73
Betrothal, 74f.
Bomor, 20
Boyanese, 3, 31, 61
Blunt, W. S., 16n.
Brooke, G. E., 90n.
Brown, C. C., 37n.
Bugis, 3

Childbirth, 89ff.
Children, custody and transfer of, 2, 111f., 126f.; socialisation and training of, 100ff.; status and treatment of, 34ff., 88, 139f.
China buta, 113f.
Chinese, 1, 3, 4, 5n., 10, 11f., 21, 93, 98, 100n.
Chuchi lantai, 91
Circumcision, 106ff.
Clitoridectomy, 107f.
Colonial Social Science Research Council, v
Conjugal relationships, 41ff., 118f.
Conversion to Islam, 11f., 99
Credit, 42

Datoek Besar, R. A., 3n.
Del Tufo, M. V., 4
Dennys, N. B., 83n.
Descent, 23
Divorce, ch. 6, 141, 147; by redemption 111; causes of and factors in, 1, 118ff., 130ff., 139; comparative data on, 134ff.; conditional, 111; economic aspects of, 123ff.; Islam and, 137ff.; legal aspects of, 110ff.; procedure, 112ff.; rate, 110, 117; repercussions of, 127ff., 139f.; revocation of, 110; *see also khula, pasah, rojo, talak*
Dress, 6f.

Economic activities, 5f.
Economic attitudes, 10f.
Economic enterprise, 46f.
Economic position of Malays, 1, 10f.
Economic relationships in the household, 41ff.
Economic relationships among kin, 2, 45ff.
Education, 8ff.
Emotional relationships in kinship, 34ff.
Evans-Pritchard, E. E., 131

Family, types of, 54ff.
Faskh, see Pasah
Fasting, 15
Fieldwork, aims and methods of, 1f.
Firth, Raymond, v, 47, 82
Firth, Rosemary, 54n., 62, 83n., 86n., 93n., 97n., 99n., 104n., 122n., 123n., 124n. 125n.
Fishing, 46f.
Fitrah, 16
Fostering, 94f.
Freedman, M., v, 12n.
Friendship, 34

Gluckman, M., 131, 134
Granqvist, H., 70f., 86n., 138
Gullick, J. M., 113n., 135

Haja, haji, 15f.
Hantar chinchin, 74f., 82
Hantar tanda, 74f.
Hari raya, 10, 36, 80, 82
Household, defined, 53; economic relationships in, 41ff.; living, 52f.; structure and composition, 53–65
Housing, 7f., 38f., 52, 62f.
Hukum, 14

Iddah, 110, 113
Imam, 15, 31
Immigrant Malays, 1, 3f., 6, 16
Indians, 1, 3, 10, 12f., 17ff.
Indonesians, *see* Immigrant Malays, Boyanese, Jayanese
Inheritance, 14f., 39ff., 45ff.
Intermarriage, 11ff., 18
Investment, 42f., 46
Islam, 15f.

Janda, 68, 78f., 82, 129
Javanese and Java, 3, 28, 61, 70, 72, 77n., 94, 96, 101n., 104n., 108, 122, 126n., 135
de Josselin de Jong, P. E., 14n.

Kathi, 15, 16, 18, 36, 67, 71, 75, 84, 111ff., 141
Khatam Koran, 107
Khula, 111, 115f., 124f.
Kin, differentiation of by children, 102f.
Kindred, 23ff.; selection within, 31ff.
Kinship, ch. 2; solidarity, 143f., 147; terminology, 22–30; *see also* Affines, Economic relationships between kin, Emotional relationships in kinship

Land ownership, 38
Lang, Olga, 50n.
Leach, E. R., 38n., 131n.
Leadership, 17ff.
Legal system, 13ff., 48
Levy, R., 112n.
Literacy, 9

Madu, 121
Mahr, 81
Makepeace, W. *et al.*, 3n.
Malay population of Singapore, 3f.
Malay Settlement, 1
Malayan dollar, value of, 9n.
Malays, definition of, 6, 16f., 21f.
Mandi mandi, 76

Mandi tolak bala, 91
Marriage, ch. 4; age at, 71; between kin, 33; ceremonies, 75ff.; consent in, 72f.; consummation of, 77; contracts, 71, 75; economic aspects of, 81f.; exchanges, 74f., 77, 78, 81, 115; expenses, 44, 74; instability of, 1, 131ff.; legal aspects of, 66ff.; preferences, 68ff., 79; procedure, 73ff.; prohibitions, 67, 69f.; proposals, 73f.; residence after, 79ff.
Mas kahwin, 81, 115f., 123f., 132f.
Masok Mělayu, 11, 99
Morris, H. S., 38n., 72n., 89n.
Mother-child relationships, 34f., 141f.
de Moubray, G. A. de C., 96n.
Muhallil, 113f.
Muslim Advisory Board, 18n.
Muslim law, 14f., 66f.
Muslims, non-Malay, 1, 2, 12f., 17ff.

Naming system, 23
Nawawi, 111
Nepotism, 49ff.
Nikah, 75, 79
Nikah gantong, 71
Nusus, 84

Occupational distribution, 1, 5f.
Orang lain, 24, 50, 70
Other Malaysians, 3, 4, 5f.

Pakistanis, *see* Indians
Parent-child relationships, 34f., 43ff.
Pasah, 111, 114, 118
Paternal and maternal kin, 32f.
Pilgrimage, 15f.
Political organisation, 17
Polygyny, 60, 64, 82ff.
Post-natal rites and ceremonies, 91f.
Potong rambut, 92
Property, ownership of, 37ff., 45ff.
Pulau Damar, 19

Radcliffe-Brown, A. R., 26n., 45n.
Raffles, Sir Stamford, 3
Residential distribution, 7
Rojo, 110, 115
Rokok daun, 10
Royal Family, Singapore, 1, 17

Saudara, 23ff., 35, 70
Sayed, 13
Schools, *see* Education

Sex ratios, 4
Sherifa, 13
Singapore Improvement Trust, 1
Singapore, population of, 3
Skeat, W. W., 91n.
Snouck Hurgronje, C., 77n.
Social Welfare Department, 55
Subandrio, H., 28n., 92n.
Swettenham, F., 3n.

Ta'alik, 111, 114, 124f.
Ta'at, 84
Talak, 110ff.
Tanjong, 1, 12n., 19f., 36, 38f., 41, 45,
    46f., 56f., 80f., 89ff., 98f., 119
Taylor, E. N., 40n., 111n., 114n., 124n.
Tĕbus talak, 111, 114, 124
Tĕngku, 17f.

Urban Malays, 7f., 21

Vesey-Fitzgerald, S., 44, 106n.
Village communities, 19ff.
Village ritual, *see Bĕla Kampong*

Wakil, 67
Wali, 67, 126
Waris, 24, 45
Weaning, 34f., 101
Wilkinson, R. J., 14n., 68n., 90n., 91n.,
    113n., 133n.
Willmott, P., 142n.
Winstedt, R. O., 10n., 40n., 80n., 89n.
Women, economic roles and rights of, 5,
    41ff., 67; status of, 142f., 128ff.

Young, M., 142n.
Yvan, Dr., 6n.

Zakat, 15f.

LONDON SCHOOL OF ECONOMICS
MONOGRAPHS ON SOCIAL ANTHROPOLOGY

Titles marked with an asterisk are now out of print. Those marked with a dagger have been reprinted in paperback editions and are only available in this form.

*1, 2. Raymond Firth, *The Work of the Gods in Tikopia*, 2 vols, 1940.

*3. E. R. Leach, *Social and Economic Organization of the Rowanduz Kurds*, 1940.

*4. E. E. Evans-Pritchard, *The Political System of the Anuak of the Anglo-Egyptian Sudan*, 1940.

5. Daryll Forde, *Marriage and the Family among the Yakö in South-Eastern Nigeria*, 1941. (Available only from International African Institute)

*6. M. M. Green, *Land Tenure of an Ibo Village in South-Eastern Nigeria*, 1941.

*7. Rosemary Firth, *Housekeeping among Malay Peasants*, 1943. (Revised edition in preparation)

*8. A. M. Ammar, *A Demographic Study of an Egyptian Province (Sharquiya)*, 1943.

*9. I. Schapera, *Tribal Legislation among the Tswana of the Bechuanaland Protectorate*, 1943. (Revised edition in preparation)

*10. W. H. Beckett, *Akokoaso: A Survey of a Gold Coast Village*, 1944.

11. I. Schapera, *The Ethnic Composition of Tswana Tribes*, 1952.

*12. Ju-K'ang T'ien, *The Chinese of Sarawak: A Study of Social Structure*, 1953.

*13. Gutorm Gjessing, *Changing Lapps*, 1954.

14. Alan J. A. Elliott, *Chinese Spirit-Medium Cults in Singapore*, 1955.

*15. Raymond Firth, *Two Studies of Kinship in London*, 1956.

16. Lucy Mair, *Studies in Applied Anthropology*, 1957.

†17. J. M. Gullick, *Indigenous Political Systems of Western Malaya*, 1958.

†18. Maurice Freedman, *Lineage Organization in Southeastern China*, 1958.

†19. Fredrik Barth, *Political Leadership among Swat Pathans*, 1959.

20. L. H. Palmier, *Social Status and Power in Java*, 1960.

†21. Judith Djamour, *Malay Kinship and Marriage in Singapore*, 1959.

22. E. R. Leach, *Rethinking Anthropology*, 1961.

23. S. M. Salim, *Marsh Dwellers of the Euphrates Delta*, 1962.

24. S. van der Sprenkel, *Legal Institutions in Manchu China*, 1962.

25. Chandra Jayawardena, *Conflict and Solidarity in a Guianese Plantation*, 1963.

26. H. Ian Hogbin, *Kinship and Marriage in a New Guinea Village*, 1963.
27. Joan Metge, *A New Maori Migration: Rural and Urban Relations in Northern New Zealand*, 1964.
28. Raymond Firth, *Essays on Social Organization and Values*, 1964.
29. M. G. Swift, *Malay Peasant Society in Jelebu*, 1965.
30. J. F. Boissevain, *Saints and Fireworks: Religion and Politics in Rural Malta*, 1965.